Especially for

Celine

Date

December 25, 2014

Love From

JN

ISBN 978-1-63058-180-0

Published by DayMaker, an imprint of Barbour Publishing, Inc., P.O. Box 719, Uhrichsville, Ohio 44683, www.barbourbooks.com

Our mission is to publish and distribute inspirational products offering exceptional value and biblical encouragement to the masses.

Printed in China.

The Woman's Secret of a Happy Life

Donna K. Maltese

DAYMAKER™
An Imprint of Barbour Publishing, Inc.

December 31

Lift up your soul and allow the power of the Holy Spirit
to lift you up in flight, knowing that the imprint of Christ
is upon you as you pray, feast upon the Word,
and wait upon the Lord. Sing a song to the Lord
in the midst of your trials, and you will be as Christ,
"sorrowful, yet always rejoicing; . . .poor,
yet making many rich; . . .having nothing,
and yet possessing all things"
(2 Corinthians 6:10 NKJV).

January 1

God's power is working in us. . . .
Our hearts ache, but we always have joy.
We are poor, but we give spiritual riches to others.
We own nothing, and yet we have everything.
2 Corinthians 6:7, 10 NLT

December 30

"Now I'm turning you over to God, our marvelous God whose gracious Word can make you into what he wants you to be and give you everything you could possibly need in this community of holy friends."

ACTS 20:32 MSG

January 2

There is a deeper happiness for Christians—one not contingent on our earthly situation. Instead it is based on a calm assurance that in spite of what is happening around us, we are trusting in Jesus, certain that the Holy Spirit is with us and that God will work all things out for our good.

December 29

Jesus, I come to You, my burdens falling off my back as I lift my eyes to the heavens. My spirit longs to feel Your presence, to see Your face, to touch the hem of Your robe. Because of Your love for me, I can rest here in You. You give me the power to live this life for You. Teach me Your way. Guide me. Whisper in my ear. Fly with me to the Father of lights.

January 3

Lord, we are women of the Way. As such, we know
that we are not to be caught up in the cares of this world but
instead filled with Your joy. Open our eyes and hearts to Your Word.
Help us to discover Your beauty in the people and things
surrounding us. Enlighten our minds, and allow
the joy we find to feed our spirits. Amen.

December 28

As we constantly take hold of our fresh mental and
spiritual attitudes, we develop a new nature,
the one God planned for in the beginning of time.
Having learned Christ, we attain new knowledge
(see Colossians 3:10) and thus attain gifts from God
(see 2 Timothy 1:6–7).

January 4

The Lord *came to help Sarah and did for her what he had promised. So she became pregnant, and at the exact time God had promised, she gave birth to a son for Abraham in his old age. . . . Sarah said, "God has brought me laughter, and everyone who hears about this will laugh with me."*

Genesis 21:1–2, 6 GW

December 27

And He raised us up together with Him and made us sit down together [giving us joint seating with Him] in the heavenly sphere [by virtue of our being] in Christ Jesus (the Messiah, the Anointed One).

EPHESIANS 2:6 AMP

January 5

Where's the proof that Jesus came to save us? That He is all-powerful? That we are more than conquerors through Him? That because of all He has done for us, we are to be filled with joy? To find the answers, we bring our thirsty hearts, minds, and souls to the source, the well of God's Word.

December 26

To increase our strength, we stay deep in God's Word and constantly renew our minds—day by day, second by second (see Romans 12:2). We do this by rejecting what the worldlings think and how they feel (see Ephesians 4:17).

January 6

Christians can be joyful because we are saved—not because we don't sin. We still miss the mark. But we can find our joy in believing that our debt for sin has been paid in full—through the death of Jesus on the cross.

December 25

As we wait upon God, we do so prayerfully (see Psalm 25:4–5), seeking His pathway for us and hoping in Him. We wait with patience (see Psalm 37:7; 145:15), not getting overanxious. We learn how to sit still and not fret over every little thing, knowing that He will provide us with the food we need, when we need it.

January 7

You were once dead because of your failures and your uncircumcised corrupt nature. But God made you alive with Christ when he forgave all our failures. He did this by erasing the charges that were brought against us by the written laws God had established. He took the charges away by nailing them to the cross.

Colossians 2:13–14 gw

December 24
For He commands and raises the stormy wind,
which lifts up the waves of the sea. . . .
He calms the storm, so that its waves are still.
Psalm 107:25, 29 NKJV

January 8

All we need to do to access that mighty power is to let Christ live through us, to trust Him with our lives, to honor Him with our mouths. We can stop cowering and instead understand that "we are more than conquerors and gain a surpassing victory through Him Who loved us" (Romans 8:37 AMP).

December 23

Somehow, Lord, I feel as if I have fallen out of my nest, my foundation in
Christ. My wings are tired, Lord, and I don't want to spiral down.
So let me stay with You for a while, resting until I can soar again.
In You, I am saved from the calamities that rush at me.
Build up my strength, Lord, as I linger here with You,
in peace and quiet, in love and trust.

January 9

My Lord Jesus, I bring myself to You today, straining to hear a whisper from Your mouth, to feel the touch of Your hand, to taste the goodness of Your Word, to see the light of Your presence in my life. I am Yours to mold and shape. Help me to become what You've called me to be, to become the vision You have had of me since the beginning. Amen.

December 22

As we learn to lean and rely upon Him, our confidence and trust build! He will be the first place we run. And there's more! The myriad of amazing promises found in Psalm 91—preservation, help, protection, renewed strength and courage, patience, hope, daily blessings, and more—can be realized only when we have determined to trust and surrender ourselves to our loving God.

January 10

I urge you. . .by the mercies of God,
to present your bodies a living and holy sacrifice,
acceptable to God, which is your spiritual service of worship.

Romans 12:1 NASB

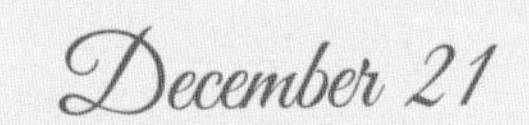

This is what the Almighty LORD, the Holy One of Israel, says:
You can be saved by returning to me. You can have rest.
You can be strong by being quiet and by trusting me.

ISAIAH 30:15 GW

January 11

Although we are weary, sorrow laden, and worn,
we know that hiding from God is not the answer.
We must and can meet God face-to-face.
Because of our faith in Jesus, we "dare to have the boldness
(courage and confidence) of free access
(an unreserved approach to God with freedom and without fear)"
(Ephesians 3:12 AMP).

December 20

As we wait upon the Lord, we are also abiding in Him, hidden in Christ. Resting in Him in that "secret place of the Most High" as Psalm 91:1 (AMP) says, we "remain stable and fixed under the shadow of the Almighty [Whose power no foe can withstand]." And the benefits in that secret place are amazing!

January 12

We can know that through thick and thin "God is on our side" (Romans 8:31 AMP), not once in a while but over and over again. Jesus "is able always to save those who come to God through him because he always lives, asking God to help them" (Hebrews 7:25 NCV). We needn't have any fear at any time!

December 19

We'll never get off the ground until we first strengthen our bodies and our wings. We do that by waiting on God as a baby eagle waits upon its parents to feed, protect, and teach it.

January 13

Weeping may last for the night, but there is a song of joy in the morning. . . . You have changed my sobbing into dancing. You have removed my sackcloth and clothed me with joy so that my soul may praise you with music and not be silent.

Psalm 30:5, 11–12 GW

December 18

"Because he has set his love upon Me, therefore I will deliver him;
I will set him on high, because he has known My name.
He shall call upon Me, and I will answer him;
I will be with him in trouble; I will deliver him and honor him.
With long life I will satisfy him, and show him My salvation."

PSALM 91:14–16 NKJV

January 14

Tell your brother Jesus all of your troubles, including sins. Tell Him you want to do better. Call on Christ's death-defying power. Count on God's protection. Follow the Holy Spirit's guidance. Sing a new song of joy unto the Lord who sees us as His dear daughters. Dance in celebration of Christ's saving grace and power.

December 17

God, thank You for sending reinforcements to watch over me. Although they are invisible, I know Your angels are forces to be reckoned with. So I will not be afraid, no matter what comes into my life. For with Your presence, the Holy Spirit's power, and Christ's love, I won't trip and fall headlong into trouble. You will keep me safe.

January 15

Heavenly Father, there are so many worldly woes tumbling around in my mind, steering my behavior, driving me out of Your path for me. Fill my mind with Your light. Help me to focus on the good things of this world—on the rose, not its thorns. For I want to know and to do Your will. I want to see Your beauty working its way out through me. Amen.

December 16

God is our Creator, source, and provider.
When we are spiritually reborn, the first thing we "see"
is Christ and His life. It is to Him we look
and to Him we become attached.
We do not instinctively know how to fly spiritually,
but we can learn by imitating Christ.

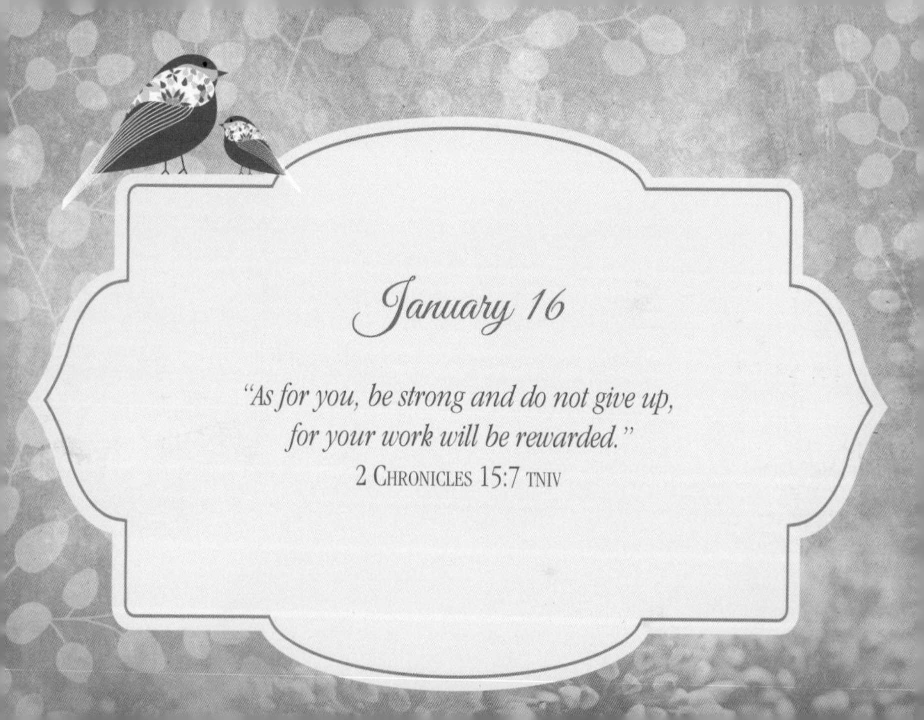

January 16

"As for you, be strong and do not give up, for your work will be rewarded."

2 CHRONICLES 15:7 TNIV

Praise the Lord*, you angels, you mighty ones who carry out his plans, listening for each of his commands. Yes, praise the* Lord*, you armies of angels who serve him and do his will!*

Psalm 103:20–21 NLT

January 17

Remember that no one can take your joy away from you (see John 16:22 NASB). Refuse to be like Hagar, sitting down in the midst of your troubles, sobbing, allowing the weight of the world's woes to oppress you.

December 14

Christ is our high place—in Him we have our foundation.
In Him we make our nest, like an eagle in the highest tree or cliff face.
As new women hidden in Christ, we are His fledglings.
Yet how do we learn to fly spiritually? The same way an eaglet does.

January 18

Just like He called Hagar, God is calling you: " 'Don't be afraid!'. . . . God opened her eyes. Then she saw a well. She filled the container with water" (Genesis 21:17, 19 GW). God is and always will be with you. Don't let your faith dry up. Run to His well and tap into His life-giving water.

December 13

We are told in 1 Corinthians 6:17 that "the person who is joined to the Lord is one spirit with him" (NLT).
We are partakers of His divine nature (see 2 Peter 1:4).
With our soul's eye on Him and our spirit joined with His, we can mount up as eagles to the highest heights, eternally secure and protected, with an open doorway to all of God's blessings.

January 19
The Lord has blessed you because you believed that he will keep his promise.
Luke 1:45 CEV

December 12

Surely He shall deliver you from the snare of the fowler and from the perilous pestilence. He shall cover you with His feathers, and under His wings you shall take refuge; His truth shall be your shield and buckler. You shall not be afraid.

PSALM 91:3–5 NKJV

January 20

In regard to the subject of God transforming us
into the image of His Son, Jesus Christ,
there are two sides—God's side and woman's side.
Simply put, God's role is to work,
and ours is to trust that He's doing it.

December 11

Lord, my eyes are looking up to You. I long to live in Your presence, in the secret place, hidden in Christ. Here with You, I am no longer afraid. I know that when I am with You, nothing and no one can hurt me. You are an amazing fortress, impenetrable. Bless my soul, Lord. I trust in You to keep me safe within Your arms and to strengthen me in Your love and light.

January 21

Lord, I'm amazed at the way You keep blessing me.
Your promises are solid. What a comfort, what a burst of confidence
I gain when I believe in You. Thank You for all You've given me in the past,
all You're giving me today, and all You've planned for me tomorrow.
You are eternal, and so is Your goodness. I bow to You today,
knowing that all good things come from You—and they are many!

December 10

God wants us to fix our soul's intellectual eye upon Him: "You will seek Me, inquire for, and require Me [as a vital necessity] and find Me when you search for Me with all your heart" (Jeremiah 29:13 AMP). In fact, we will be blessed with joy and peace—even amid the storms—when we do so (see Jeremiah 17:7).

O LORD, You are our Father; we are the clay,
and You our potter; and all we are the work of Your hand.

ISAIAH 64:8 NKJV

December 9

He who dwells in the secret place of the Most High shall abide under the shadow of the Almighty. I will say of the Lord, *"He is my refuge and my fortress; my God, in Him I will trust."*

Psalm 91:1–2 NKJV

January 23

God has given us the Word to live by.
He has given us the power of prayer.
He has told us that He loves us.
And now we are to be further shaped—by His
transforming power—from lumps of clay into vessels
"unto honour, sanctified, and meet for the master's use,
and prepared unto every good work"
(2 Timothy 2:21 KJV).

December 8

Take each juggernaut event in your life—big or little—and gird yourself in the Word, open your spiritual eyes, and board the chariot for your soul. Allow your chariot to take you to the heavenly places where you can "ride prosperously" (Psalm 45:4 NKJV) with God on top of all, allowing you to triumph within and without!

January 24

We have been pulled up out of the miry clay pit and put into God's hands.
Overjoyed at our coming to Him, He begins to shift our shapes,
to pull us apart, to knead us, to mold us.
Our role is to remain still, patient, and pliable.

December 7

Do not allow the juggernauts of this world to roll over you and sink you into the pits of despair, desperation, and fear. Instead, mount up with God, taking each offense, bitter word, tragedy, loss, trial, and temptation as your chariot of God that will take you to the "heavenly places in Christ Jesus" (Ephesians 2:6 KJV).

January 25

God began doing a good work in you,
and I am sure he will continue it until it is finished.

PHILIPPIANS 1:6 NCV

December 6

O our God, . . .we have no might to stand against this great company that is coming against us. We do not know what to do, but our eyes are upon You.

2 Chronicles 20:12 AMP

January 26

When we step out of the boat and head to Jesus' side,
we are putting ourselves in His hands.
But when we look away from Him
and stare at the wind and waves,
we are no longer trusting in or focusing on Jesus.
Then, like Peter, we begin to sink.

December 5

Lord, hear my cry! Come rescue me. Reach down from above and pull me out of this trouble. My heart is heavy, Lord. I can hardly move. Rescue me, for I feel as if I am drowning in a sea of difficulties. I long to rest in You, to hear Your voice, to feel Your touch. I have eyes of faith, Lord. Reveal Your chariot and whisk me away!

January 27

Lord, I seek Your kingdom. I seek Your face, Your presence, Your Word. Each day brings me closer and closer to what You would have me be. Each day I rise to new challenges, knowing that You are walking with me every step of the way. I have confidence that You are designing me for something special. May who I am glorify You!

December 4

Anything we rely on other than God will, at some point, be taken away. Hannah Whitall Smith wrote, "God is obliged often to destroy all our own earthly chariots before He can bring us to the point of mounting into His." He longs to have us depend on Him more than anything or anyone else. For He was, is, and will be the only One we can truly depend on.

January 28

His divine power has given us everything we need for a godly life through our knowledge of him who called us by his own glory and goodness. Through these he has given us his very great and precious promises, so that through them you may participate in the divine nature.

2 PETER 1:3–4 TNIV

December 3

I called on the Lord *in my distress. I cried to my God for help. He heard my voice from his temple, and my cry for help reached his ears. . . . He spread apart the heavens and came down with a dark cloud under his feet. He rode on one of the angels as he flew, and he soared on the wings of the wind. . . . He reached down from high above and took hold of me. He pulled me out of the raging water. He rescued me from my strong enemy.*

Psalm 18:6, 9–10, 16–17 GW

January 29

God forbid we should be found wanting and remain lumps of clay. Or that we miss out on what grand plans God has in store for us because we've sunk down into the dark and deep blue sea!

December 2

We will not prosper if we look to an earthly conveyance to help us through. For God has told us, "Woe to them that go down to Egypt for help; and stay on horses, and trust in chariots" (Isaiah 31:1 KJV).

January 30

We lumps of clay will not be transformed into vessels overnight.
It will take many spins of the Potter's wheel.
But we can rest assured that we are safer in His hands
than in a deep, dark pit, that although we may experience
growing pains, we will someday be mature Christians,
energized and transformed by the Holy Spirit.

December 1

In the temporal world, our chariots don't seem like they are paved
with love. Instead they often appear very unattractive.
Slights from people we once considered friends.
Betrayals by loved ones. The cruelties of neglect, greed,
malice, and selfishness practiced in the world.
Yet every chariot sent by God (whether of first or second cause)
must be paved with love, for our "God is love"
(1 John 4:8 KJV).

January 31

People won't receive God's approval by their own efforts. . . .
Christ came so that we could receive God's approval by faith. . . .
In our spiritual nature, faith causes us to wait eagerly
for the confidence that comes with God's approval. . . .
What matters is a faith that expresses itself through love. . . .
What matters is being a new creation.

GALATIANS 2:16; 3:24; 5:5–6; 6:15 GW

November 30

O Lord my God, You are very great. . . .
He makes the clouds His chariot;
He walks upon the wings of the wind.
Psalm 104:1, 3 NASB

February 1

We need not stress ourselves out with trying
to help God transform us.
That's like the batter attempting to help
the baker make it into a cake. It just doesn't happen.
All the batter can do is keep on trusting
and surrendering to its designer.
We also need not try to tell our Creator what
we think we should be and do.

November 29

Show me the true reality, Lord. Reveal Your chariot for me so that I can rise above this world. Remove the scales of worldly woes from my eyes. Open my eyes to the fact that You will never leave me defenseless. Give me twenty-twenty spiritual vision. Your army of hosts is always here to lift me up, into the heavens. Save me, Lord. Beam me up now!

February 2

Sometimes my ego wants to take over, Lord. I want to take myself out of Your hands and attempt my transformation in my own power. But it's exhausting! I feel weak and spent. Renew my patience, Lord. Help me to persevere. Lead me to see myself through Your eyes—a work in progress—with the end goal of glorifying You.

November 28

We must quiet ourselves by vision.
Elisha knew by faith that he was safe from the Syrian forces.
But he knew his servant was very troubled. So he prayed for him.
" 'Lord, I pray, open his eyes that he may see' " (2 Kings 6:17 NKJV).
And so the Lord did. The servant's eyes of faith
were opened to God's multitude of chariots!
This is the prayer we must pray,
that God would open our spiritual eyes.

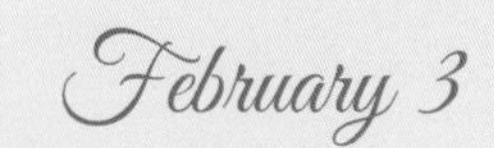

"Grow up. You're kingdom subjects.
Now live like it. Live out your God-created identity.
Live generously and graciously toward others,
the way God lives toward you."

MATTHEW 5:48 MSG

November 27

"Don't be afraid!" Elisha told him.
"For there are more on our side than on theirs!"
Then Elisha prayed, "O Lord, open his eyes and let him see!"
The Lord opened the young man's eyes, and when he looked up,
he saw that the hillside around Elisha was filled
with horses and chariots of fire.

2 Kings 6:16–17 NLT

February 4

Although it is God who is actually doing the work
of transformation as we yield ourselves to Him,
we are to keep up our faith and belief that He is indeed doing so.
To shore up that trust in Him, we can turn to God's Word
and embed it in our hearts. We can lift our faith
by practicing prayer and find ourselves buoyed
by remaining in His presence.

November 26

Like Elisha, we have a choice. We can allow our juggernauts—big or little—to crush us, plunging us down into fear, defeat, and despair, or we can jump into the chariots of God and rise above them in triumph. All the losses, trials, minor irritations, worries, and woes that come to us become chariots the moment we treat them as such.

February 5

Have you drifted out of the Potter's hands?
Has impatience driven you to work in your own power?
If so, surrender yourself on the altar. Put yourself back into God's hands
and await His working in your life. He will transform you into
the image of Christ "from glory to glory" (2 Corinthians 3:18 KJV).

November 25

Elisha did not fear his enemies because he walked by faith—
not by sight! He knew God would protect him,
that when—not *if*—he prayed, God would send His forces.
"The chariots of God are twenty thousand,
even thousands of thousands" (Psalm 68:17 NKJV)!

February 6

Hosea put it well: I'll call nobodies and make them somebodies;
I'll call the unloved and make them beloved.
In the place where they yelled out, "You're nobody!"
they're calling you "God's living children."

Romans 9:25–26 MSG

"In the wilderness. . .you saw how the Lord your God carried you,
as a father carries his son, all the way you went
until you reached this place."

Deuteronomy 1:31 TNIV

February 7

The true Christian life is best described as the life "hidden with Christ in God" (Colossians 3:3 NASB). Unlike the usual Christian experience, in which we believe and have been saved but do not exhibit Christlikeness, the so-called higher Christian life is described in the Bible as one of continual rest in Jesus, of peace that surpasses all understanding. It's calm assurance and abundant joy in the midst of trials and chaos.

November 23

Lord, I thank You for bringing me new life in Christ. I am setting my sights on Your heavenly kingdom. These troubles here on earth will be but a dim memory someday. So instead of wallowing in self-pity or trying to fix situations on my own, I am going to journey inward to Your side, knowing that when I do, You will give me the strength and peace I crave.

February 8

I am amazed, Lord, that You would take notice of me.
I am thrilled that in Your eyes I am a somebody who is loved.
I rejoice in the fact that I am Your living daughter.
I have faith in Your process. I have faith in Your vision for me.
May I bring You the glory You deserve, in this life and beyond.

November 22

Often our earthly woes don't at all resemble God's chariots.
Instead, they manifest themselves as stresses, heartaches, disputes,
trials, offenses, misunderstandings, losses, and callousness. . . .
But if, like Elisha, we could see these woes as God's vehicles
of victory, we would rise above these cares in triumph,
attaining heights we never dreamed possible!

February 9

But Zion said, "I don't get it. Gᴏᴅ *has left me.*
My Master has forgotten I even exist."
"Can a mother forget the infant at her breast,
walk away from the baby she bore?
But even if mothers forget, I'd never forget you—never."

Isaiah 49:14–15 msg

November 21

*Since you have been raised to new life with Christ,
set your sights on the realities of heaven, where Christ sits
in the place of honor at God's right hand.*

COLOSSIANS 3:1 NLT

February 10

God will never forget us. He is always listening,
waiting for us to share and let go of all our burdens—
the greatest of which is self. Often we are so focused
on our feelings, our unique temperaments,
our own peccadilloes and temptations, our expectations,
fears, and plans that we cannot see clearly.
We allow these things to take over our thoughts,
to hold us in bondage.
But our selves must be abandoned to God.

November 20

Do not fear. Christ has been with you all along.
He is ready to help you rest in Him. Allow Him to carry all your burdens,
give you insights that only He would have, and empower you to live your
life to the fullest 24–7. This is what you have been created for.
For it is not you who lives, but Christ lives in you.

February 11

We are to give God all our other burdens—of health, Christian service, careers, husbands, children, households, friends—everything that produces those horrible worry lines. Often we are so consumed with the worries of this world that we lose our focus on God.

November 19

God wants us to come to Him willingly.
We are already His living temple. Christ already resides in us,
and we already received the Holy Spirit when we accepted Christ.
What we need to do is continually, consistently,
and completely *recognize* Christ's presence within us
and *surrender* ourselves to Him.

You will keep in perfect peace all who trust in you,
all whose thoughts are fixed on you!

Isaiah 26:3 NLT

November 18

All praise to God, the Father of our Lord Jesus Christ, who has blessed us with every spiritual blessing in the heavenly realms because we are united with Christ.

Ephesians 1:3 NLT

February 13

Make Jesus your security blanket.
Whatever your issue—yourself, your plans,
your husband, your children, your work,
the world's woes, your misgivings, apprehensions,
or anxiety—take it to your Lord.
Reach out for His garment.
By faith, allow Him to take your burden upon Him
and leave you whole.

November 17

Lord, I know I am not to believe my feelings. I am not to use them as a barometer of my life hidden with You. But I need Your help today. Let me rest in Your arms. Allow me to just lean back and let You take over. Show me the true way, the true life—that You and I are one, the perfect union. Keep me focused on You and Your love.

February 14

Lord, I am weary of worrying about everything.
My emotions are as volatile as the stock market.
So I come to You today, ready to unburden myself.
I lay my plans, my loved ones, my life at Your feet.
In exchange, I pick up Your peace, love, kindness,
and strength, confident that You do all things well.

November 16

How wonderful to have a joy that is not tied to what happens
to us throughout our days. Knowing that Christ is
loving us within and sheltering us without,
that no one can truly harm us,
is contentment at its best.

February 15

Do not let your hearts be troubled, neither let them be afraid. [Stop allowing yourselves to be agitated and disturbed; and do not permit yourselves to be fearful and intimidated and cowardly and unsettled.]

John 14:27 AMP

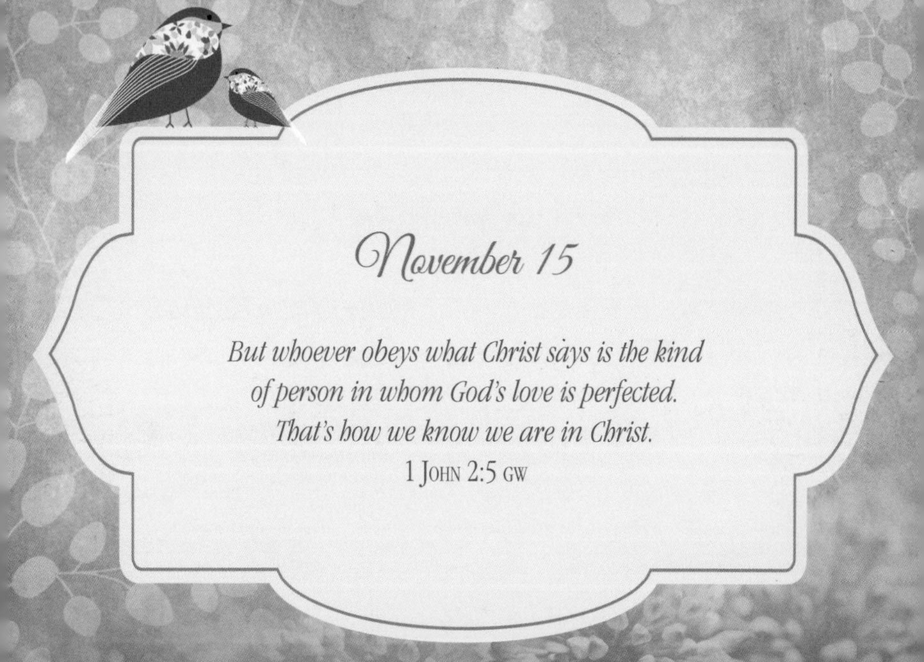

November 15

But whoever obeys what Christ says is the kind of person in whom God's love is perfected. That's how we know we are in Christ.

1 John 2:5 GW

February 16

Be calm. Be carefree. Become an assured daughter of God, knowing that He will never leave you. He will never forget you. He has "written your name on the palms" of His hands (Isaiah 49:16 NIRV).

November 14

Those living in the full power of a union with Christ have natures that are loving, joyful, peaceful, long-suffering, kind, good, faithful, gentle, and have self-control (see Galatians 5:22–23). Because you are fully aware that He is living through you, you won't be able to be anything but, for you have become "partakers of the divine nature" (2 Peter 1:4 NASB).

February 17

We are to live "careful for nothing" (Philippians 4:6 KJV). Let go of the past, present, and future. God has promised to take care of you. It's not a theory, but fact! Look to the lilies and the birds. If God is taking care of them, He is more than attentive to what those created in His image need, want, desire, and deal with, every moment of every day.

November 13

When we consciously and consistently recognize Christ within, the evidence of this union comes through in the form of our character. For when we are truly, fully, and intimately one with Christ—allowing Him to have complete and utter reign over us—we are Christlike, for "anyone who claims to be intimate with God ought to live the same kind of life Jesus lived" (1 John 2:6 MSG).

February 18

"Give your entire attention to what God is doing right now, and don't get worked up about what may or may not happen tomorrow. God will help you deal with whatever hard things come up when the time comes."

MATTHEW 6:34 MSG

November 12

God chose him as your ransom long before the world began, but he has now revealed him to you in these last days.

1 Peter 1:20 NLT

February 19

In regard to our cares, it is not our circumstances
that need altering. It is we ourselves.
It is our mind-set that must first be shifted.
Then the conditions will naturally be changed.
With a simple, childlike faith in God who sees all
and knows all, our whole world—indeed
our entire outlook—changes.

November 11

Each day, Lord, I remember that it is You living within me.
Each hour I surrender myself to Your leading and love.
Each moment I sense Your power to rise above this world.
The true reality is our divine blending. May I rest in the peace
that You are always with me, working through me,
loving me—a new world without end, amen.

February 20

I have decided that I'm going to stop thinking about what may or may not happen today and tomorrow, God. Instead I am going to rest assured that no matter what difficulties may arise, all is well. You will help me through the conflict as I pray my way through. I rejoice at the challenges before me, knowing that with You on my side, I need not fear anything!

November 10

Dwelling within you, a true believer, is the Spirit of Christ.
You are a temple of the living God.
And if you read to whom this applies, you'll see that
this scripture pertains to "mere infants [in the new life] in Christ"
(1 Corinthians 3:1 AMP) who are still being fed with milk!
So this is not a new dimension to your life as a believer.
Christ has been residing in you all along!

February 21

Jesus heard what they said, and he said to Jairus, "Don't worry. Just have faith!"

MARK 5:36 CEV

November 9

Put on the new self, which in the likeness of God has been created in righteousness and holiness of the truth.

Ephesians 4:24 NASB

February 22

The Lord Himself gave a wonderful analogy in
Matthew 18:2–3, saying that unless we "become as little children,"
we will not be able to "enter into the kingdom of heaven" (KJV).
Remember your years as a little child? As a child,
you provided nothing for yourself,
yet whatever you needed was provided.
You didn't worry about tomorrow but lived in the now.

November 8

God has not made our union with Him difficult, nor has He kept it a secret. Yet some of us may not yet completely grasp the concept of being fully one with God. Perhaps our hearts do not fully believe it is available to us. Or we may be afraid to trust Him totally. Yet that is where this entire pathway of Christian life is leading to—*voluntarily* embracing a full oneness with God.

February 23

Like a nursing mother, when God hears your every sigh,
whine, and cry, He responds immediately.
You are His precious baby girl. Trust Him as you trust the earth
to support you. You are in His hands, heart, and thoughts.
It is in Christ Jesus—who does all things well—
that you will find your peace and rest.

November 7

God's entire plan for us "before the foundation of the world" (1 Peter 1:20 NASB) was for our souls and spirits to be united with our ultimate Bridegroom. This divine union is what Jesus prayed for—and not just for His disciples but for us, those who would later come to believe in Him.

February 24

Open my eyes so I can see what you show me of your miracle-wonders.

Psalm 119:18 MSG

November 6

The spiritual nature produces love, joy, peace, patience, kindness, goodness, faithfulness, gentleness, and self-control.

GALATIANS 5:22–23 GW

February 25

The true Christian experience is not something we can achieve
by any sort of directed effort on our part.
Rather, it is something we gain possession of by receiving it,
as we would a gift from a loved one.

November 5

I want to partake of Your divine nature, God. So I come to You, surrendering all that I am. I know Your Holy Spirit is within me, a gift from You. So I now give You a gift in return—*all* my heart, mind, body, and soul. Take possession of me, Lord. I am opening the door to You. Shine Your light throughout my being. Warm me with Your love. Illuminate me!

February 26

Open my eyes, mind, heart, and spirit, Jesus, so I can see how wonderful my life is hidden in You. I want to know You, feel Your presence. I want to do what You would have me do. I want to love others as I love myself. Teach me, show me, give me Your vision. Enlighten me so that I may not be afraid but give myself to You willingly—moment by moment.

November 4

God is the One who can rescue us from the poverty of ashes
and the tower of temptation. With His kiss, we are awakened
to a new reality. On Him alone can we rely, for He will never leave us.
He is our comfort, peace, and rock.
He is the One with whom we want to become one
and live happily ever after.

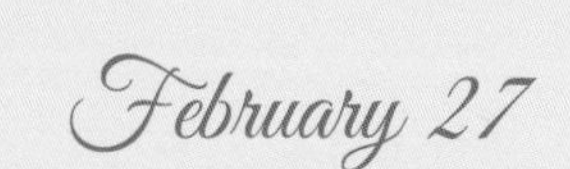

Roll your works upon the Lord [commit and trust them wholly to Him; He will cause your thoughts to become agreeable to His will, and] so shall your plans be established and succeed.

PROVERBS 16:3 AMP

November 3
You surely know that your body is a temple where the Holy Spirit lives.
The Spirit is in you and is a gift from God.
You are no longer your own.
1 Corinthians 6:19 CEV

February 28

A child does not earn affection from its mother.
Instead, it receives something the mother can't help but give.
So does our Father God give us this life,
as a gift He can't help but express to us.
Our only role is to receive the good and perfect gift
(see James 1:17) of Christ Jesus in God
with a thankful heart from His loving hand.

November 2

Your love and devotion to Him is all the Lord asks of you as a reward for all He has done for you. Let yourself go—your entire self—mind, body, soul, strength, talents, spirit, everything you are! Lay it all before Him.

March 1

We must put ourselves entirely in His hands and allow Him to have His way with us—no matter how we feel or what we judge to be right! This will inevitably lead to a life of blessings and peace in Christ, for God the Father only wants what is best for us.

November 1

In this loving relationship with Christ, God may at times be silent.
This is a sign of the intimacy we have with Him,
like an old couple who sit quietly together, at times,
comfortable in each other's silent presence.
This may be a moment in which we must patiently await
His next message, content with remaining
with Him and meditating on His Word.

March 2

I will not be afraid, because the LORD *is with me.*
People can't do anything to me.

PSALM 118:6 NCV

October 31

Your written instructions are miraculous.
That is why I obey them. Your word is a doorway that lets in light,
and it helps gullible people understand. I open my mouth
and pant because I long for your commandments.

PSALM 119:129–131 GW

March 3

Is it not true that God Himself is so much more loving to us
than we could ever be to one cherished individual?
Isn't He the One who gave us His one and only Son
to save us from our sins? To save us from ourselves?
In fact, He is just aching for us to enter not only
the kingdom of God but the kingdom of heaven.

October 30

To have the faith of Noah, to build a huge ark in the desert,
to ignore the heckling of worldlings as he goes out on a limb
in obedience to You—that's the courage I'd like to have.
For when we step out in faith, obeying everything You ask us to do,
You work miracles, saving more than just us but also others in our lives.
I want to be that intimate with You, Lord. Pull me close. I will obey.

March 4

Hidden in You, Jesus, I have nothing to fear. No one can touch me. Your love and presence, Your strength and truth shield me from whatever weapons this world can use against me. How wonderful to have such protection! How glorious to have such courage in You. I can face anything within the One who will never leave me.

October 29

If only our desire to chase after God would be
as great as our desire for a new pair of shoes or a purse!
If you do not yet have that desire, pray that
God would grant you passion for His Word,
understanding of His love, and a desire
to follow Him with everything you are!

March 5

Nothing now, nothing in the future, no powers, nothing above us, nothing below us, nor anything else in the whole world will ever be able to separate us from the love of God that is in Christ Jesus our Lord.

Romans 8:38–39 NCV

October 28

By faith, Noah built a ship in the middle of dry land.
He was warned about something he couldn't see,
and acted on what he was told. The result? His family was saved.
His act of faith drew a sharp line between the evil of the
unbelieving world and the rightness of the believing world.
As a result, Noah became intimate with God.

HEBREWS 11:7 MSG

March 6

Our words to our loving God must be "Thy will be done."
And in order to say that, we must have faith—
an essential element necessary to receive any gift.
Nothing—especially that which is purely mental or spiritual—
ever really becomes ours until we believe it has been given
wholeheartedly and then claim it as our own precious gift.

October 27

With Him as our foundation, obeying Him and His Word every moment of every day, we will be able to keep our heads in times of temptation or persecution. We will keep our comfort, hope, peace, and joy in the midst of distressing situations; and we will be kept spurred on by His amazing power!

March 7

Remember how much Christ loves us and how we cannot be separated from that love? Remember how much He has forgiven us? Unless we believe in this love and forgiveness, and claim both as our own, they are not really ours.

October 26

How wonderful that He so desires us to rely on Him instead of ourselves! He has such joy in our response to Him as our true love! It is beyond our understanding. He is continually knocking on our door, hoping we will let Him in (see Revelation 3:20).

March 8

[God] did not spare his own Son but gave him for us all. So with Jesus, God will surely give us all things.

Romans 8:32 NCV

October 25

If you [really] love Me, you will keep (obey) My commands.
And I will ask the Father, and He will give you another Comforter
(Counselor, Helper, Intercessor, Advocate, Strengthener, and Standby),
that He may remain with you forever.

John 14:15–16 AMP

March 9

In Christ, we taste the joy of the kingdom of heaven.
He is that "pearl of great price" (Matthew 13:46 KJV),
our hidden treasure (see Matthew 13:44).
He is the well of living water (see John 4:14)
we so desperately thirst for and to which
we may continually come.

October 24

Wow! Being overtaken by blessings is a mind-boggling image.
To imagine that You are already working on my future blessings before
I've even said, "Here I am, Lord! Ready, willing, and able to do as You ask!"
What a concept! Your promises make me so eager to obey.
So I come to You today, Lord, to await Your orders.
My heart is wholly dedicated to Your desires.

March 10

Jesus, I can't imagine how broken God's heart was when He sacrificed You,
His one and only Son, for me. Such love is unfathomable,
yet such love is mine. And surely as I remain hidden in You,
Jesus, God will withhold nothing else.
Everything that is good and right will be met in my life.
Thank You for saving me. Make my life something special for You.

October 23

Jesus makes this offer of an intimate, loving relationship to all who will say yes to Him, but all do not accept His invitation. Other interests and loves (of others or self) are too precious for some to cast aside. The future of heaven is still available to them, but they will miss out on the unfathomable joy of this present moment!

March 11

By his divine power, God has given us everything we need for living a godly life. We have received all of this by coming to know him, the one who called us to himself by means of his marvelous glory and excellence. And because of his glory and excellence, he has given us great and precious promises. These are the promises that enable you to share his divine nature and escape the world's corruption caused by human desires.

2 Peter 1:3–4 NLT

October 22

"And all these blessings shall come upon you and overtake you, because you obey the voice of the Lord *your God."*

Deuteronomy 28:2 NKJV

March 12

John Greenleaf Whittier wrote,
"The steps of faith fall on the seeming void,
but find the rock beneath." Christ is a mighty Rock
on which we stand in this life and the next.
So don't be afraid to take these steps of faith.
With Him beneath us, we will not sink in the sand
but stand triumphant upon our Lord and Master.

October 21

This privilege of surrender is one that is not demanded by God. It is a matter of our choice, part of our free will. But not abandoning ourselves to Him will keep us from having the joy of the Lord, for Jesus has said, "Blessed (happy and to be envied) rather are those who hear the Word of God and obey and practice it!" (Luke 11:28 AMP).

March 13

With God in our corner, His courage and strength in our hearts,
and ourselves hidden in Christ, we have assurance
that we can indeed cross that river
and make it into the Promised Land.

October 20

Although you do not yet know it, when you surrender yourself to Christ and obey Him in everything, you will be fulfilling your spiritual destiny. In wholly binding your life to Him, you will discover the reality of the Almighty God! You will be walking in light, not darkness.

March 14

You are holy. . . . But you must continue to believe this truth and stand firmly in it. Don't drift away from the assurance you received when you heard the Good News.

Colossians 1:22–23 NLT

October 19

As a young man marries a young woman,
so will your Builder marry you; as a bridegroom rejoices
over his bride, so will your God rejoice over you.

Isaiah 62:5 TNIV

March 15

When we base the truth of God and our commitment
on what we feel—or don't feel—we are misdirected,
thinking that perhaps we have not given ourselves over to God at all.
Since our feelings belie the truth—that we have indeed
committed heart, body, mind, and soul over to God—
we cannot believe that He has us in His hands.

October 18

I love You so much, Lord, and although I don't always understand what is happening, I know You will work everything out. All I need to do is stay focused on You and obey all Your commands. For I am here to love You with all my heart, mind, body, soul, and strength and to love others as myself. Serving You is a glorious mission. I want no other master!

March 16

Dearest Jesus, I feel treasured that You have chosen me,
set me apart to be holy. Increase my faith, Lord.
Remind me every day that I am Your saint.
Assure me with Your Gospel truths.
Plant them in my heart so that I will not waver
from the path You have chosen for me.
Help me be the woman You have called me to be.

October 17

It seems too risky, too difficult,
too scary for you to give Him all He asks.
You see others going through this life without even acknowledging
His presence, and they seem to be getting along just fine.
So why must you surrender yourself to the nth degree
to this Son of God called Jesus?
Ask Him to place understanding in your heart today.

March 17

"Nothing that a man irrevocably devotes to God from what belongs to him. . .may be either sold or bought back. Everything devoted is holy to the highest degree; it's God's inalienable property."

Leviticus 27:28 MSG

October 16

And we know that all things work together for good to those who love God, to those who are the called according to His purpose.

Romans 8:28 NKJV

March 18

The way to meet the challenge of consecration, to give yourself entirely to God, is to get in line with God's order of things—fact, faith, and only then feeling. Are you afraid to turn yourself over completely to God's will? Afraid of losing your personality, which you may have grown fond of over the years? You need not be!

October 15

Move forward in the power of quietness, knowing that God surrounds you, Christ is within you, and the Holy Spirit guides you. Recognize that your energies should not be used exclusively to pursue worldly means but to seek first His kingdom, knowing that He will provide whatever you need.

March 19

So be courageous. Take the step. Turn yourself over to God.
Then consider it a fact that you are His.
He has accepted you—lock, stock, and barrel.
Allow your faith to kick in.
Know that you are in His hands,
that He will work through you to do His will.

October 14

A simple Christianity, where we seek truth, strive to serve others, and do God's will is more important now than ever before. The only solution to the emptiness of our lives, the seemingly ever-present threat of terrorism, and the fruitlessness of living in a society that seeks only to have more and then more is a transparent Christianity where others look at us and see Christ alone.

March 20

Doing whatever you feel like whenever you feel like it,
and grabbing whatever attracts your fancy.
That's a life shaped by things and feelings instead of by God.

COLOSSIANS 3:5 MSG

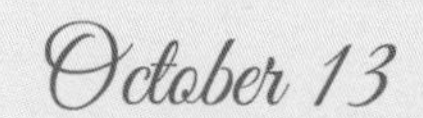

Be gentle and forbearing with one another and, if one has a difference (a grievance or complaint) against another, readily pardoning each other; even as the Lord has [freely] forgiven you, so must you also [forgive].

Colossians 3:13 AMP

March 21

As the days go by, don't give in to the idea that nothing has really changed after all just because you don't *feel* it. This kind of wrestling will go on and on unless you cut it short by faith.

October 12

Lord, my mind-set is totally off today, and I haven't even gotten out of bed yet. So I will be still before You, practicing the presence of God. You are now here. I pray for Your spiritual vision. I reach out with faith that You will do what You have promised to do. I leave my life, my regrets, my work in Your hands, knowing You will provide all I need every moment of this day.

March 22

Lord, I find it so easy to give in to my feelings.
The next thing I know, I've distanced myself from You.
Yet I long to be so close to You in every way in every moment of the day.
Help me to obey You, not give in to whatever mood overtakes me.
Give me Your peace in this process, reminding me that I am a work
in progress but headed in the right direction—to Your side.

October 11

Many times it is better to be a woman of few words. Proverbs 17:28 tells us that "even fools are thought wise if they keep silent, and discerning if they hold their tongues" (TNIV).

March 23

I also pray that you will understand the incredible greatness of God's power for us who believe him. This is the same mighty power that raised Christ from the dead and seated him in the place of honor at God's right hand in the heavenly realms.

Ephesians 1:19–20 NLT

Set your minds and keep them set on what is above (the higher things), not on the things that are on the earth.

Colossians 3:2 AMP

March 24

Remember that our thoughts fuel our feelings,
and our feelings orchestrate our actions.
So if we do not feel consecrated to God,
we will certainly not act like it.

October 9

David Hume has said that "he is happy whose circumstances suit his temper; but he is more excellent who can suit his temper to any circumstance." How true! Here we must reflect, asking ourselves if our good temper remains, no matter what.

March 25

Because God has done it all and made you holy,
His work is what is going to change your behavior.
His power is going to change your life.
Since God has already done it,
why are you wearing yourself out trying to live right?
And why, if you are misbehaving,
are you acting as if He hasn't done anything at all?

October 8

We will not be plagued with anxieties or what-ifs,
because we know that only today is ours.
God has given it to us from His loving hand.
He has taken back all our yesterdays,
and all our tomorrows are still in His hands.
We will live happily in the consciousness of here and now.

March 26

I pray that your hearts will be flooded with light so that you can understand the confident hope he has given to those he called—his holy people who are his rich and glorious inheritance.

Ephesians 1:18 NLT

October 7

Your old life is dead. Your new life, which is your real life—even though invisible to spectators—is with Christ in God. He is your life. When Christ (your real life, remember) shows up again on this earth, you'll show up, too—the real you, the glorious you. Meanwhile, be content with obscurity, like Christ.

COLOSSIANS 3:3–4 MSG

March 27

God has made you a new woman in Christ (see Colossians 3:10)!
You have been designed to be what He wants you to be!
And through the power of the Holy Spirit,
God has given you the same power and the same strength
as Christ, to be that new woman.

October 6

Lord, I have surrendered myself to You. I want to follow Your path,
not that of the world. Make me humble, gentle, and honest.
Help me to forgive others, to love all, to seek You first above all things.
Give me the strength to be not like this world but like You.
For You are the true treasure hidden within me,
the source of all power as You work through me to reach all.

March 28

Flood my heart with Your light, Jesus. Help me tap into Your power.
Lead me to understanding and being confident in the hope
You have given me. As a daughter of the King, I am rich in everything.
And I thank You for allowing me to be a part of God's family,
for calling me into Your kingdom—all to Your glory!

October 5

With Christ's mantle without, the Spirit's power within,
and God's presence surrounding each of us here and now,
we will be expressing our Lord and Savior to everyone we meet!
We will find ourselves walking as Christ walked.
We will be a peculiar people—empowered, loving,
keeping no record of wrongs, returning evil with good,
gentle, meek, kind, and yielding.

March 29

The grace (blessing and favor) of the Lord Jesus Christ (the Messiah) be with all the saints (God's holy people, those set apart for God, to be, as it were, exclusively His). Amen (so let it be)!

REVELATION 22:21 AMP

October 4

If we say we are his, we must follow the example of Christ.

1 JOHN 2:6 CEV

March 30

Being a saint, being *consecrated*, isn't based on our feelings or our behavior. It's based on the power God has given us as we have fully committed ourselves to Him. He will work through us, to help us walk as Christ did, if we just believe. For that we need faith and prayer.

October 3

If we are to be Christians who walk the walk and talk the talk, we had best be hidden in Christ 24–7—not just in front of other believers and the minister, but at home, at work, everywhere we go, and in everything we do!

March 31

To make our prayers more effective, we need to believe
that God is real—even though He is not visible to our human eyes.
We must believe the fact that His presence is a certain thing and
that He sees everything we do and hears everything we say.
This takes the faith described in Hebrews 11:1—
"the substance of things hoped for, the evidence of things not seen" (NKJV).

October 2

Although you may not be a professional preacher,
your life, your words, and your behavior do demonstrate
to others what you believe. If you call yourself a Christian,
when others see you they should see Christ, for
"clearly you are an epistle of Christ"
(2 Corinthians 3:3 NKJV).

April 1

And though you have not seen Him, you love Him,
and though you do not see Him now, but believe in Him,
you greatly rejoice with joy inexpressible and full of glory.

1 PETER 1:8 NASB

We have the mind of Christ (the Messiah) and do hold the thoughts (feelings and purposes) of His heart.

1 Corinthians 2:16 AMP

April 2

Most times, faith is something that keeps us looking to the Lord during times of trial, knowing that we can trust the One who knows so much better than we do. Faith is what we rely on when our non-Christian friends jeer at our naiveté.

September 30

Because of You, Lord, I know I need never be afraid of anyone or anything in this world. You are great, mighty, powerful, and it is to You—and not the things or people of this world—to whom I pledge my undying faith. I refuse to be caught up in the competition for affluence, to worship the almighty dollar. Instead, I come to You, my Master, seated in the heavens.

April 3

Lord, I long to be like Abraham, who
"by faith. . .obeyed when God called him" and
"went without knowing where he was going" (Hebrews 11:8 NLT).
Although I have never seen You in Your physical form,
I love You and believe in You with all my heart, mind, body,
and soul. Lead me on to the place You have for me.
I trust You with my life—today, tomorrow, and forever.

September 29

We who have determined to live the higher life,
a life hidden in Christ, should be as a result of that life a "peculiar people" (1 Peter 2:9 KJV)—not conformed to this world but transformed by the renewing of our minds (see Romans 12:2) each and every day!

Things that are seen don't last forever,
but things that are not seen are eternal.
That's why we keep our minds on the things that cannot be seen.

2 Corinthians 4:18 CEV

September 28

Light, space, zest—that's God! So, with him on my side I'm fearless, afraid of no one and nothing.

Psalm 27:1 msg

April 5

This Savior of ours is the One who stilled the wind and the waves, who brought dead people back to life, who changed water into wine, and healed the blind, deaf, and dumb. He is the One who Himself rose from the dead—just to save us!

September 27

Through all your endeavors, be sure that God and His will are your motivating powers. Plug in to His Word to keep you fit and nourished, unfettered of stress, and free of worry. Continually seek His guidance and direction through prayer, then exercise your faith by taking bold steps where no woman has ever gone before—for God's glory and His glory alone.

April 6

It's amazing how much we trust our fellow humans and how little we trust God. When we fly in planes, we trust the pilot to deliver us safely to our destination. When we head to our favorite restaurant, we expect a good meal, not even considering that the chef could serve us salmonella-laced chicken.

September 26

You are accountable for doing what God has called you to do
and what He has given you the talents to perform—
nothing more and nothing less. Remember that the work is God's,
that He gives to each "according to his [or her] ability"
(Matthew 25:15 TNIV). What a relief that the work is God's—
and you are just His instrument!

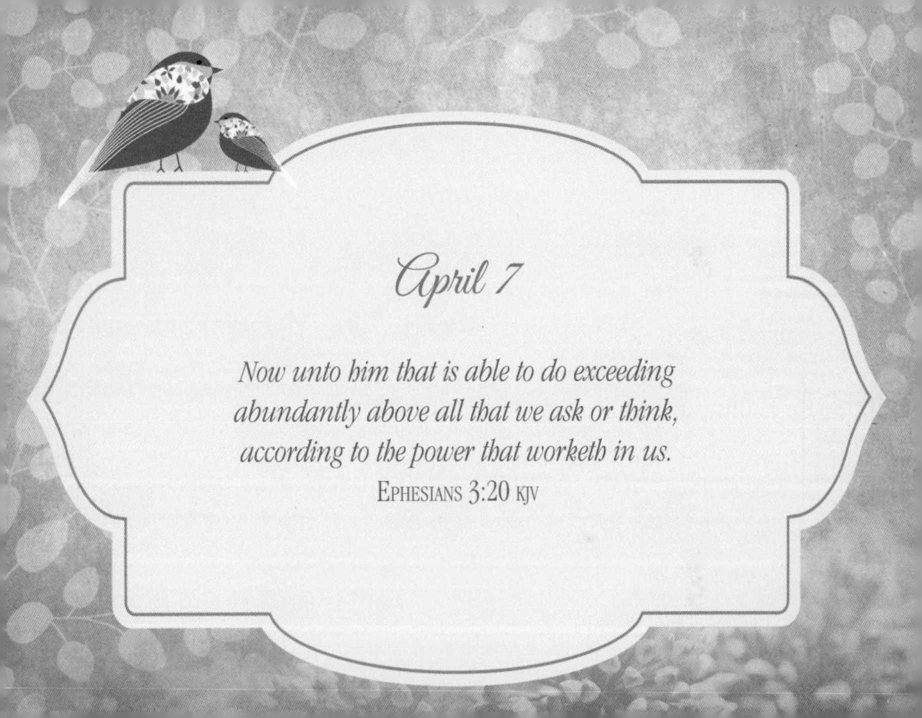

April 7

Now unto him that is able to do exceeding abundantly above all that we ask or think, according to the power that worketh in us.

Ephesians 3:20 KJV

September 25

To break through despair, cultivate joy within yourself. Recognize that God has a plan for your life, " 'plans to prosper you and not to harm you, plans to give you hope and a future' " (Jeremiah 29:11 TNIV). Take joy in that promise!

"Well done, good and faithful servant! You have been faithful with a few things; I will put you in charge of many things. Come and share your master's happiness!"

MATTHEW 25:21 TNIV

April 8

How can we have faith in strangers, who are only human,
yet not have faith in God—the One who
has power over all creation?
And how can we have faith that other places
on this planet exist without our ever having seen them,
yet not have faith that God actually exists?

September 24

I need Your courage, Lord. Like Esther, I am really stepping out, taking a major leap of faith. Remind me that the success of all my works is in Your hands, not mine. So I give the actual work, the strength to accomplish it, and its results to You. And I take up the mantle of Your peace, power, and perseverance to achieve what You're leading me to do.

April 9

Lord, I feel like I have been fishing forever yet haven't caught anything because I've been trying to do it in my own power and wisdom. So as Your disciples did, I turn to You, believing You will direct me to the right spot. I know that by trusting in You, my net will wind up so full of fish that I will not be able to "drag it up into the boat" (John 21:6 CEV). What a miracle of faith!

September 23

Instead of giving up, lean harder on God.
He will see you through! It's the evil one who is
pointing out all your faults and feeding your misgivings.
Pray, and trust God to give you persistence
as well as the courage and care you need.

April 10

It was by faith that even Sarah was able to have a child,
though she was barren and was too old.
She believed that God would keep his promise.

HEBREWS 11:11 NLT

"Who knows whether you have not come to the kingdom for such a time as this?"

Esther 4:14 ESV

April 11

Our thoughts lead us astray. We must continually look to God's Word, write it upon our hearts, and believe that He will do as He has promised. We must imprint the words of Hebrews 11:1 upon our minds: "Now faith is the assurance (the confirmation, the title deed) of the things [we] hope for, being the proof of things [we] do not see and the conviction of their reality [faith perceiving as real fact what is not revealed to the senses]" (AMP).

September 21

The remedy is to get our eyes off ourselves and back on God. "And whatever you do, do it heartily, as to the Lord and not to men, knowing that from the Lord you will receive the reward of the inheritance; for you serve the Lord Christ" (Colossians 3:23–24 NKJV). We are to be not human pleasers but God pleasers. Forget self.

April 12

Perhaps you think you lack faith because you don't feel the working of the Holy Spirit in your life. In believing this you have, in effect, not only made God out to be a liar and called false the "record that God gave of his Son" (1 John 5:10 KJV), but you have also lost any confidence in the Holy Spirit. In this regard, the fault lies in your lack of faith in God and His Word, not in the power of the Holy Spirit.

September 20

One bondage of service is doing things to exalt ourselves or with the expectation of receiving an external reward. With that kind of pressure, no wonder many Christian workers fall by the wayside. They are so anxious to do something well and right to impress people that they find themselves filled with worry. These kinds of efforts detract from Jesus. If you are exalting yourself, you have taken the glory from Christ.

April 13

We don't yet see things clearly. We're squinting in a fog, peering through a mist. But it won't be long before the weather clears and the sun shines bright! We'll see it all then, see it all as clearly as God sees us, knowing him directly just as he knows us!

1 Corinthians 13:12 msg

September 19

As each has received a gift, use it to serve one another,
as good stewards of God's varied grace: whoever speaks,
as one who speaks oracles of God; whoever serves,
as one who serves by the strength that God supplies—in order
that in everything God may be glorified through Jesus Christ.

1 Peter 4:10–11 ESV

April 14

Put your thoughts, then, over onto the side of faith.
Say to yourself, *Lord, I will believe.*
I do believe, over and over again.
Replace every suggestion of doubt—from within
or without—with a statement of faith until,
whether facing triumph or trial,
you stand firm in your faith.

September 18

Serving You can be done in so many different ways, Lord. I love giving little secret blessings to those I encounter in my daily endeavors, knowing that You are interested in the little things as well as the big. So each day, Lord, point out to me whom You would like me to secretly serve. Whisper in my ear how You would like me to bless them. And thank You for the joy this brings!

April 15

Lord, I can't see the forest for the trees.
My mind is tempted to focus on a myriad of what-ifs.
I can't imagine how You will straighten out this mess.
But I refuse to worry. Instead, I will trust in You.
I will not fret but stand firm in faith, no matter how circumstances seem.
I refuse to go by feelings. Instead, I will rest in the strength of
Your wisdom and the comfort of Your loving arms.

September 17

We can't believe that God has called us to join the worship team, serve on the church board, or head the committee for vacation Bible school. What we need to understand is that God has already gone before us and prepared the way for us (see John 10:3–4). The way to break through is to build up our God-confidence by nurturing our spirits in the Word. We must read His promises, His truths, and apply them to our hearts.

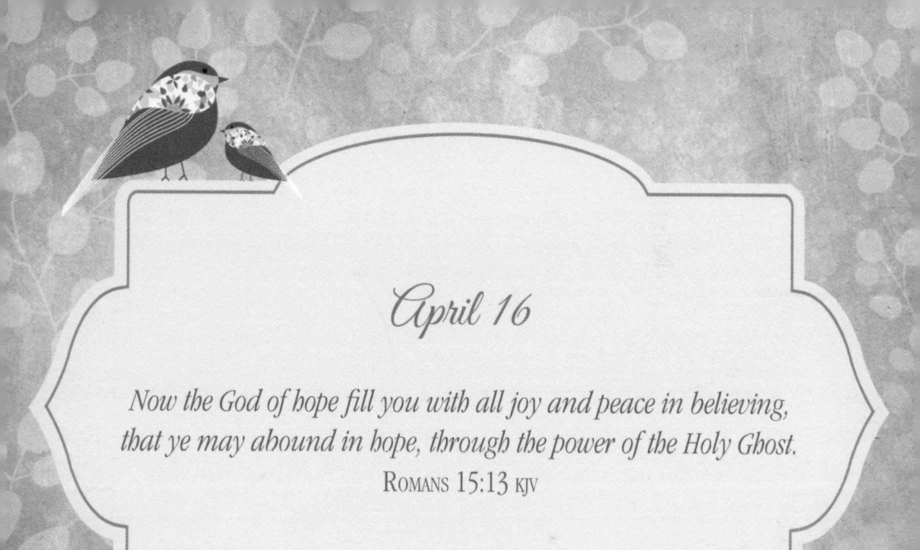

April 16

Now the God of hope fill you with all joy and peace in believing, that ye may abound in hope, through the power of the Holy Ghost.

ROMANS 15:13 KJV

September 16

When you give to the poor, don't let anyone know about it.
Then your gift will be given in secret.
Your Father knows what is done in secret,
and he will reward you.

MATTHEW 6:3–4 CEV

April 17

When panic knocks on your door, answer it with unswerving
trust in the Lord. Speak to it with God's words of faith.
Reach for His calm, for His peace.
Don't allow fear and the panicked thump of your heart
to drown out the words God is speaking into your life.
Banish discouragement—lack of courage—
for it is a major impediment to your union with God.

September 15

To break through this bondage of flagging energy and desire to do God's work, we must go to prayer. Ask God to help you to understand that He has given you the energy and desire to do what He has called you to do. Envision that He is filling you up with everything you need to do the job. Recognize that your strength is your biggest weakness.

April 18

Stop your frenzied activity. Take a few deep breaths.
Look into God's Word.
Allow it to penetrate your spirit, soul, and mind.
Write it upon your heart.
As you build up your faith, peace will pervade.

September 14

Sometimes we feel as if we are no longer strong
enough to accomplish what God has asked us to do.
So we either do it begrudgingly or not at all.
Yet the fact of the matter is that God has intended us
to do what He wills, for He has written it upon our hearts
and planted the seeds within our minds
as part of His new covenant with us
(see Hebrews 8:10).

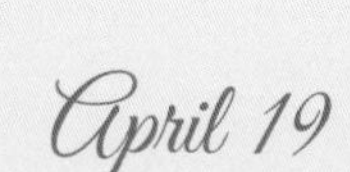

In Christ we were chosen to be God's people,
because from the very beginning God had decided
this in keeping with his plan.
And he is the One who makes everything agree
with what he decides and wants.

EPHESIANS 1:11 NCV

September 13

He calleth his own sheep by name, and leadeth them out. And when he putteth forth his own sheep, he goeth before them, and the sheep follow him: for they know his voice.

John 10:3–4 KJV

April 20

Once we saints have stepped out in faith,
trusting God as we live hidden in Christ and beginning
to perceive the blessings of such a union,
another challenge meets us on our soul's pathway.
Although we have tasted Christ's peace and rest,
both may begin to wane as we wonder if
we are truly walking in God's will.

September 12

Jesus, Your grace and love are overwhelming.
You give me the strength to do all that You have called me to do.
Your power shines through my weakness. I am envisioning Your strength
and power resting over me like a tent. There is nothing I cannot do!
This is a truth that I will emblazon on my heart, for it will give me
peace and confidence as I do Your will to Your glory!

April 21

I may not understand all You are doing, Lord, or why,
but I rest secure in the knowledge that You have a plan for all of us.
I am in harmony with You, Lord, ready and willing to do what You would
have me do. Your wisdom out-trumps my erratic emotions, God.
So I am realigning myself with Your will and Your wonderful ways!

September 11

When we feel anxious, beleaguered, disdainful, exhausted,
and tied up in knots about our Christian work, or when
we have an impending desire to find our way out of serving others,
we can be sure we have stepped off our pathway and
embarked upon a route of bondage.
We must immediately step back and look at our situation
with the means of breaking through to receive
the power that awaits women hidden in Christ.

April 22

We pray that you will lead a life that is worthy of the Lord. We pray that you will please him in every way. So we want you to bear fruit in every good thing you do. We want you to grow to know God better. We want you to be very strong, in keeping with his glorious power. We want you to be patient. Never give up. Be joyful.

Colossians 1:10–11 NIrV

September 10

But He said to me, My grace (My favor and loving-kindness and mercy) is enough for you [sufficient against any danger and enables you to bear the trouble manfully]; for My strength and power are made perfect (fulfilled and completed) and show themselves most effective in [your] weakness. Therefore, I will all the more gladly glory in my weaknesses and infirmities, that the strength and power of Christ (the Messiah) may rest (yes, may pitch a tent over and dwell) upon me!

2 Corinthians 12:9 AMP

April 23

We begin to think we have not dug deep enough, we are not wholly God's—thus, we are not holy; we are nothing more than pretenders. At this point, we have once again begun to rely upon our emotions instead of the truth of God. If we consider that the life hidden in Christ is lived in the things we feel, all our attention is focused on our emotions rather than where it belongs—on Christ.

September 9

As God makes the baby grow without it even being aware that it is indeed growing, He has planted us to grow spiritually. And we are utterly helpless to do anything but allow Him to do so, and not hinder His work within us. For when we hinder Him, we expend all our energy, grow exhausted, and suddenly find ourselves growing backward rather than forward. We would be wise to tap into the lily's secret and grow in God's way.

April 24

When we are at our lowest point, we feel we may not have surrendered ourselves to God's will at all. At this juncture, we must fall back upon the truth that life in Christ is not lived in the emotions but in the will. And if we keep our will consistently abiding in its center—which is God's will, the true reality—our emotional ups and downs will not disturb us.

September 8

If we expend effort trying to make ourselves
grow spiritually, fussing and straining at every turn,
our fruit will bear witness to our unnecessary toiling.
We will be burned out—a common malady in church workers.
We will wilt under stress. We will look for relief
in all the wrong places instead of turning to God.
Our eyes will be on our own selves or our self-dependence
and self-effort. Place your eyes on Christ today.

April 25

[We] refute arguments and theories and reasonings and every proud and lofty thing that sets itself up against the [true] knowledge of God; and we lead every thought and purpose away captive into the obedience of Christ (the Messiah, the Anointed One).

2 Corinthians 10:5 AMP

September 7

And He [Jesus] said to me,
"My grace is sufficient for you,
for My strength is made perfect in weakness."
Therefore most gladly I will rather boast in my infirmities,
that the power of Christ may rest upon me.

2 Corinthians 12:9 NKJV

April 26

We must realize that when we are not walking in God's will, there is dissonance. For only when our will is tied to His, and His will obeyed, will harmony reign within us. That is when the Holy Spirit truly begins to gently guide us into right living.

September 6

Father God, there have been times I have worried about my finances. But living a life hidden with Your Son, I am putting those anxieties behind me and resting in You. I know the plans You have for me are for hope and a future. Thus, I will flourish as You would have me do. Thank You for loving me so. Thank You for always watching over me.

April 27

Father God, everybody is talking at me.
But I don't hear a word they're saying;
I hear only Your voice of wisdom.
I am filling my heart and mind with Your wonderfully wise Word—
so there's no room for doubt or confusion, panic or fear.
I bring every thought to Christ, knowing He will replace it with Your truths.
In Him I have freedom to be what You would have me be!

September 5

To be like the lily, you must understand
that you have not chosen Christ, but He has chosen you.
He says that He has "[planted you], that you might go
and bear fruit and keep on bearing" (John 15:16 AMP).
That is how we got into His grace in the first place!
So He has planted us as He has the lily,
which revels in and responds
to God's sunshine, water, and soil.

April 28

Ask and keep on asking and it shall be given you;
seek and keep on seeking and you shall find;
knock and keep on knocking and the door shall be opened to you.
For everyone who asks and keeps on asking receives;
and he who seeks and keeps on seeking finds;
and to him who knocks and keeps on knocking,
the door shall be opened.

LUKE 11:9–10 AMP

September 4

He who leans on, trusts in, and is confident in his riches shall fall,
but the [uncompromisingly] righteous
shall flourish like a green bough.

Proverbs 11:28 amp

April 29

Although our emotions belong to us and are tolerated
and enjoyed by us, they are not our true selves.
They are not who we actually are.
Thus, if our God is to take hold of us,
it must be into this central will or personality that He enters.
Then if He is reigning within that central
will by the power of His Spirit,
all the rest of that personality
must come under His influence.

September 3

To grow in grace, our souls must be planted in the very heart of God's love.
We must steep ourselves in grace and allow it to surround us.
God has it in His plan that we grow in such a way.
We are to "consider the lilies of the field and learn thoroughly
how they grow; they neither toil nor spin. Yet I tell you,
even Solomon in all his magnificence (excellence, dignity, and grace)
was not arrayed like one of these" (Matthew 6:28–29 AMP).

April 30

We must again shift our will to the believing side.
For when we choose to *believe*, we need not worry about how we *feel*.
Your emotions will eventually be compelled to come into
the harmony of the real you, the woman hidden in Christ,
in the secret place of the Father!

September 2

In order to grow in grace, we have to plant ourselves in it,
allowing our roots to go deep into this life hidden in Christ.
Once we do, our spiritual growth will take off,
and we will progress beyond our imagination.

God, see what is in my heart.
Know what is there. Put me to the test.
Know what I'm thinking.
See if there's anything in my life you don't like.
Help me live in the way that is always right.
PSALM 139:23–24 NIrV

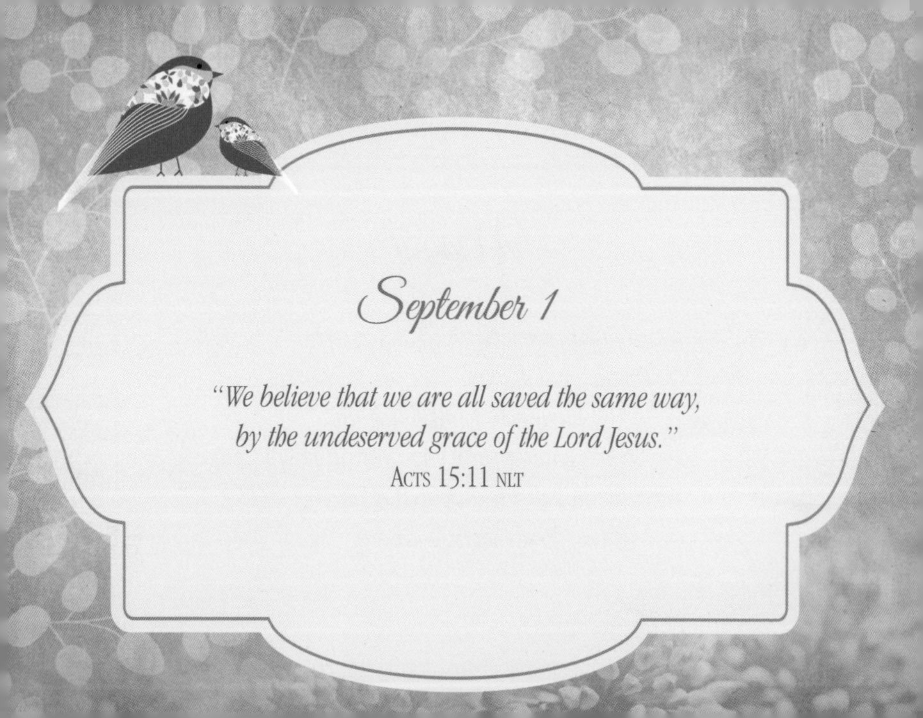

September 1

"We believe that we are all saved the same way, by the undeserved grace of the Lord Jesus."

Acts 15:11 NLT

May 2

At times, we find great difficulty in controlling our emotions,
a well-known fact to the majority of females.
But we *can* control our will.
So we may say firmly and continually,
"I give my will to God."
For deep inside, we know He *always* knows best.

August 31

Every day I am becoming more and more of what You want me to be, Father God. When my emotions threaten to take control, I "consider the lilies" (see Matthew 6:28; Luke 12:27), and Your peace immediately enters in. I am focusing on You, Jesus, knowing that's what I need to do. In You is where I crave to be. Because once I've experienced growth in grace, it becomes a magnificent obsession.

May 3

Abba, my spirit seems in dissonance with Yours.
I'm feeling stress and anxiety in my heart,
which makes me think I'm listening to the enemy's lies.
But that's not what You want for me, so please,
Father God, give me a heart check today.
Make me aware of anything I am doing that is not of Your will.
Bring me back in line with You.
I long for the peace of living in Your will.

August 30

Earthly parents become alarmed and seek medical advice
if their babies do not grow physically. So would God our Father
be alarmed if we, His children, do not continue to grow spiritually.
Yet many of us feel as if we can accomplish this growth
in our own power. Perhaps we believe that if we try to do greater
and greater things, we will reach the epitome of spirituality.
Yet like the flowers and trees, we cannot *make* ourselves grow.
That job has been left in the hands of our Father.

May 4

If any of you lack wisdom, let him ask of God, that giveth to all men liberally, and upbraideth not; and it shall be given him.

James 1:5 KJV

August 29

And God is able to make all grace abound toward you, that you, always having all sufficiency in all things, may have an abundance for every good work.

2 Corinthians 9:8 NKJV

May 5

All we need to do is seek God's kingdom first;
everything else will fall in line!
When we live in God's will and are hidden in Christ,
we take up residence in the worry-free zone,
a place where emotions amount to naught,
where they become mere specks of dust floating
on the surfaces of our minds.

August 28

As we grow up in Christ, embarking on the pathway God has marked out for us, He intends for us not to stagnate like the Dead Sea but to flow ever on to the place He bids us, nestled deep in His grace. We are not to have our flow impeded by getting hung up on our faults and failings. Instead, we can simply perceive any growing pains resulting from our missteps and imperfections as blessings, because for us who have not yet arrived, it's all about the journey.

May 6

In the midst of our daily activities, we, too,
do not need to know or understand all that God is doing.
We need merely to take a step back and focus on Jesus.
We need not fear God's will but trust Him,
resting in the truth that He knows what He's doing.

August 27

We can banish the grief, shame, self-doubt,
and self-condemnation that come upon us when we make
choices that have led us in the wrong direction.
These missteps are merely part of our growth process.
Thus, we should take care not to succumb to constant
and consistent thoughts of our failings.

May 7

Your ears shall hear a word behind you, saying,
"This is the way, walk in it," whenever you turn
to the right hand or whenever you turn to the left.

ISAIAH 30:21 NKJV

August 26

But the apostles stayed there a long time, preaching boldly about the grace of the Lord. And the Lord proved their message was true by giving them power to do miraculous signs and wonders.

Acts 14:3 NLT

May 8

You are on the initial steps of the pathway to a life of faith.
You have given yourself to God—mind, body, soul, and spirit.
You are in His hands, and He is shaping you
into a new creature with a divine purpose.
You have determined to keep your will in agreement with His.
You are, in effect, trusting Him with everything.

August 25

Lord, I find such joy in Your wonderful gift of grace. I know that what is happening around me is not as significant as what is going on *within* me. I am rooting myself—heart, body, soul, and mind—in Your soil of grace. I look only to You to meet all my needs. So doing gives me an abundance of peace I have never known before. Thank You, Lord, for Your amazing grace!

May 9

Lord, I long to hear Your voice whisper in my ear.
I need Your guidance, Your direction.
Be my compass, for I don't know which way to go.
Lead me out of the darkness I feel surrounding me.
Help me look away from my emotions and focus on You and You alone.
Lead me on. But if I need to wait, give me patience to do just that.

August 24

If we look at ourselves and the people around us,
we can see that everyone is in a different stage of growth in a myriad of areas. In this journey through life, we are all working at becoming what we believe God has called us to be.
And because we are still works in process,
in the midst of growth, not one of us is perfect.

May 10

If any of you is deficient in wisdom, let him ask of the giving God [Who gives] to everyone liberally and ungrudgingly, without reproaching or faultfinding, and it will be given him.

James 1:5 AMP

August 23

Blessed (happy, enviably fortunate, and spiritually prosperous—possessing the happiness produced by the experience of God's favor and especially conditioned by the revelation of His grace, regardless of their outward conditions) are the pure in heart, for they shall see God!

MATTHEW 5:8 AMP

May 11

With the Father, Son, and Holy Spirit on your side,
you cannot get lost. You need not fear anything!
If you confidently believe in God the Father; His Son, Jesus;
and the Holy Spirit, if you determine to look for
and expect their guidance, you will receive it.

August 22

With our adoring eyes upon our Father—not on ourselves, others, or material things—we can relax. So rest in Daddy God. Recognize that you are His child, a beautiful daughter and heir, a free woman, a new creature in Christ. Allow His Spirit to have His way. Sit back and leave the driving to Him. And let the fun—and joy—begin!

May 12

God will give you guidance if you seek it in faith,
with confidence that He will give it. In addition,
you must keep in mind that God knows absolutely everything!
So regardless of how you or those around you see confusion
and loss in the path He has chosen for you,
He knows exactly what blessings await.

August 21

If we keep in mind how God views us,
we will bear the fruit of His Spirit—"love, joy, peace, patience, kindness, goodness, faithfulness, gentleness and self-control. Against such things there is no law" (Galatians 5:22–23 TNIV).

May 13

If you do what the Lord *wants,*
he will make certain each step you take is sure.
The Lord *will hold your hand,*
and if you stumble, you still won't fall.

Psalm 37:23–24 CEV

August 20

"I am the Alpha and the Omega, the Beginning and the End. To the thirsty I will give water without cost from the spring of the water of life. Those who are victorious will inherit all this, and I will be their God and they will be my children."

REVELATION 21:6–7 TNIV

Although you may not understand His road map for you,
remember that with your human vision,
you see only a portion of the map.
He sees the entire picture, and in His vision you must trust.

August 19

I come to You today, Lord, with all the love in my heart.
The core of my spirit melts in adoration of You.
My mind is not on earthly things but on the one thing that will get
me through this life, this day, this moment—love for my Father God.
In these moments, as I bask in my love for You, I find I am made whole
and overflowing with love for others and myself. What amazing love!

May 15

I'm hanging on to You for dear life, Abba. Keep a tight grip on me.
Squeeze my hand if I'm walking out of Your will for me.
I don't want to stray, for whenever I step out on my own,
I always trip up. But You'll never let me fall.
You are my refuge and my strength.
You are my guiding light.
So I'm determined to stick to You like glue
and to praise Your name with each step!

August 18

The secret to our freedom is to be as God sees us—
as little children. "You are no longer slaves,
but God's children; and since you are his child,
he has made you also heirs" (Galatians 4:7 TNIV).
Get God's view of you set in your mind.
Walk as if you are a daughter of the King—
because you are!

May 16

Thus says the Lord: Stand by the roads and look;
and ask for the eternal paths, where the good, old way is;
then walk in it, and you will find rest for your souls.

Jeremiah 6:16 AMP

August 17

" 'So love the Lord your God with all your heart, with all your soul, with all your mind, and with all your strength.' The second most important commandment is this: 'Love your neighbor as you love yourself.' No other commandment is greater than these."

MARK12: 30–32 GW

May 17

But how does God give us His guidance?
In four simple ways: through His Word,
through providential circumstances, through our
spiritually enlightened judgment, and through
the inward promptings of the Holy Spirit upon our minds.
When these four harmonize, when they are all in sync,
we know God's hand is guiding us.

August 16

God's law told us where we were falling short (see Galatians 3:24–25). And although it served to bring us to Christ (see Galatians 3:24–25), it can never save us. Only Christ can do that.

May 18

If your road map bypasses scripture,
beware—you are headed for a dead end.
If you are confused about which path to take,
you are directed to consult God's Word (see 2 Timothy 3:16–17).
If the Bible provides guidance in that particular regard,
ask the Holy Spirit to make everything clear to you. Then obey.

August 15

How exhausting to live in bondage!
Thank God Christ came to save us from the law of Moses,
for there was no way we could satisfy its demands.
Instead, He gave us two new laws to replace all others:
"Love the Lord your God with all your heart and with all your soul
and with all your mind (intellect). This is the great
(most important, principal) and first commandment.
And a second is like it: You shall love your neighbor as
[you do] yourself" (Matthew 22:37–39 AMP).

May 19

Wait and hope for and expect the Lord; be brave and of good courage and let your heart be stout and enduring. Yes, wait for and hope for and expect the Lord.

Psalm 27:14 AMP

August 14

[Jesus] said, "I tell you the truth, unless you turn from your sins and become like little children, you will never get into the Kingdom of Heaven."

MATTHEW 18:3 NLT

May 20

If our circumstances are truly providential,
God will open doors for us—we won't have to break them down.
In other words, if our direction is truly from God,
He will go before us and pave the way.

August 13

Father God, I am so wrapped up in works and my own
self-interest that I have lost my footing on Your pathway.
My free spirit is snared in these earthly trappings.
I know my ego and my spirit are like oil and water—they do not mix!
So help me, Jesus, not to live according to my feelings
but according to my faith. Break these chains, Lord.
I now claim the freedom found only in You.

May 21

I seem to be in limbo, Lord, waiting for Your direction.
Right now all is unclear. But all that means is that
You want me to be patient until You give me the signal.
I know You only want what's best for me.
So my hope and trust are in You. Show me,
Lord—via the scriptures, my intelligence, Your voice,
and the Spirit's prompting—when and where to move.

August 12

As spiritually reborn children of God's promise, we freedwomen cannot go back to lives of slavery under the law! Remember, Ishmael was sent away once the promised son had arrived—because law and grace cannot exist together!

May 22

For You are my rock and my fortress;
for Your name's sake You will lead me and guide me.

Psalm 31:3 NASB

August 11

Live freely, animated and motivated by God's Spirit. Then you won't feed the compulsions of selfishness. For there is a root of sinful self-interest in us that is at odds with a free spirit, just as the free spirit is incompatible with selfishness. These two ways of life are antithetical, so that you cannot live at times one way and at times another way according to how you feel on any given day. Why don't you choose to be led by the Spirit and so escape the erratic compulsions of a law-dominated existence?

GALATIANS 5:16–18 MSG

May 23

It's not enough to feel you are being led
to a new endeavor or action.
You must discern the source of the voice calling you
before you rush off down the path. Step back.
Take the time to find the true voice—
no matter how long you may have to wait.
Listen carefully.

August 10

Make this clear in your mind: God is not so much interested in what you *do* as He is in what you *are*. God has His eye on your inner woman, the new creature born when you first accepted Christ.

May 24

Endeavor to discern God's guidance by using what Hannah Whitall Smith calls "a divine sense of 'oughtness' derived from the harmony of all God's voices." When you do, you will have nothing to fear. If you have faith in Him, if you trust Him with all, you will have the courage and strength to walk the way He is leading, your hand in His.

August 9

The true pathway is that of the free woman and should be the route of all Christians. But sadly, once we have begun our initial walk, we are often led astray, falling back into our former life of bondage to the world. Ask the heavenly Father to keep you on the right path.

May 25

I rise before the dawning of the morning, and cry for help;
I hope in Your word. My eyes are awake through the night watches,
that I may meditate on Your word.
Hear my voice according to Your lovingkindness;
O Lord, revive me according to Your justice.

Psalm 119:147–149 NKJV

August 8

To me, though I am the very least of all the saints (God's consecrated people), this grace (favor, privilege) was granted and graciously entrusted: to proclaim to the Gentiles the unending (boundless, fathomless, incalculable, and exhaustless) riches of Christ [wealth which no human being could have searched out].

EPHESIANS 3:8 AMP

May 26

Christians are sometimes called believers because
we have faith in God. We do not doubt that He exists.
But many of us could be called doubters because
we do not have an active, personal relationship with Christ.
We are perhaps not even certain God likes us, much less loves us.
We hesitate to say that we have been forgiven totally,
that our destiny is indeed heaven.

August 7

Lord, I feel like such a fool. I've been trying to become perfect by *doing* things. But the reality is that all I need to do is *be* Your daughter. Help me to live my life as Your servant—not as a slave to the law. You are to be my main focus—not the approval of others, not my pride. I want to walk in freedom and in Your Spirit. I want to live for You—and You alone!

May 27

Here I am, Lord, coming to You bright and early,
before my feet hit the floor. I am hoping in Your Word,
Lord, knowing that is what will protect me
from the doubts that threaten to rise within my mind.
I know You have given me the keys to Your kingdom.
I am Your daughter, so there is no need to fear.
You will do as You have promised. And I rejoice in that fact!

August 6

Christian women have a choice.
We can live in bondage, or we can experience
the freedom that life in Christ affords.

May 28

"God is not like people. He tells no lies.
He is not like humans. He doesn't change his mind.
When he says something, he does it.
When he makes a promise, he keeps it."

NUMBERS 23:19 GW

August 5

After starting your Christian lives in the Spirit, why are you now trying to become perfect by your own human effort? Have you experienced so much for nothing? Surely it was not in vain, was it? I ask you again, does God give you the Holy Spirit and work miracles among you because you obey the law? Of course not! It is because you believe the message you heard about Christ.

GALATIANS 3:3–5 NLT

May 29

The instant we let doubts enter our mind,
our fight of faith ends and our spiritual rebellion begins.
In fact, when we doubt, we are calling God, Jesus,
and the Holy Spirit liars, for "he that believeth not
God hath made him a liar" (1 John 5:10 KJV)!
What sorrow we must give our Abba God.

August 4

We need not enjoy our trials but simply understand
that we must trust God's will, wisdom, and creativity in the midst of them
and impress the certainty upon our minds that He is with us
through it all until the end of the age (see Matthew 28:20).
Knowing this, we can simply let go with abandon and let God work
His marvels in good times and bad, praising Him all the way.

May 30

Perhaps you feel unworthy of receiving the promises of God.
Perhaps temptations have gotten the best of you;
you have sinned to the point of believing God would be well rid of you.
After all, why should He have any love for an undeserving sinner such as you?
Perhaps you have undergone numerous trials that
have convinced you that for some reason God has forsaken you
and no longer cares about you or your life.
Share your doubts with the heavenly Father right now.

August 3

Our God is an awesome God! He leads us through desert places.
But if we keep our eyes on His pillar of light and follow
the cloud He sends before us, we will have the living water
we need to continue along the way.
He will provide us with manna—His wonderful Word.

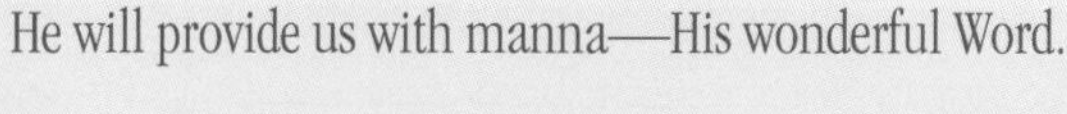

May 31

But if any of you lacks wisdom, let him ask of God, who gives to all generously and without reproach, and it will be given to him. But he must ask in faith without any doubting, for the one who doubts is like the surf of the sea, driven and tossed by the wind.

James 1:5–6 NASB

August 2

Always be joyful. Never stop praying.
Whatever happens, give thanks, because it is
God's will in Christ Jesus that you do this.
1 THESSALONIANS 5:16–18 GW

June 1

If you have entertained doubts, be assured:
God came to save us. In fact, He has told us that He
"came not to call the righteous, but sinners to repentance"
(Luke 5:32 KJV). Hannah Whitall Smith wrote,
"Your very sinfulness and unworthiness, instead of being
a reason why He should not love you and care for you,
are really your chief claim upon His love and His care!"
What a wonderful truth to meditate on.

August 1

I'm determined to rejoice in the midst of this trial, Lord.
Through my tears and pain, I give You praise and sing Your name.
In this life, Lord, I want to glorify You. You will give me the strength
and courage to face anything—any man, woman, or child.
Through You I can love them unconditionally
and forgive any misdeeds. Praise, praise, praise!

June 2

Lord, You know what frightens me.
You know what doubts assail me and make me feel like
I'm sinking in quicksand. So I ask You today, Lord, as I read Your good
Word, to lead me to a promise I need to learn, memorize, and carve into
my heart. I need Your wisdom to lead me into the light of understanding.
Shine Your Word on me, Lord. I am ready!

July 31

God is not the author of sin, but He uses His creativity and His wisdom to work the design of His providence to His—and our—advantage. All we need to do is trust Him to work things out to our good. He will overrule events, trials, and tragedies in our lives to His glory and our praise!

Commit thy way unto the Lord; trust also in him;
and he shall bring it to pass.
And he shall bring forth thy righteousness
as the light, and thy judgment as the noonday.
Rest in the Lord, and wait patiently for him: fret not.

Psalm 37:5–7 KJV

July 30

While Joseph was in prison, the Lord was with him. The Lord reached out to him with his unchanging love and gave him protection. . . . The Lord was with Joseph and made whatever he did successful.

Genesis 39:20–21, 23 gw

June 4

We are not perfect; yet in spite of our faults,
while we are still a long way off, our Father God sees us
and is "moved with pity and tenderness" for us.
He runs to us, embraces us, and kisses us "fervently"
(Luke 15:20 AMP). Then He celebrates our return!
This happens each time we stray.

July 29

We are like a child in God's arms.
Everything that touches us goes through Him first.
We must realize that no evil exists—no matter how dark
and bleak—that God cannot turn into good.

June 5

We have " 'complete and free access to God's kingdom,
keys to open any and every door: no more barriers between heaven
and earth, earth and heaven' " (Matthew 16:19 MSG).
So rid yourself of any doubts, which only lead to despair.
Sink your teeth into God's promises. He already knows all about you.
He's known you since before you were born!

July 28

In all things we must be patient and totally abandoned to God's will and way, to His plan for us, through every blessing as well as every trial. For God loved Jesus as much on the cross as He did on Mount Tabor (where Jesus was transfigured).

June 6

I cried out, "I am slipping!"
but your unfailing love, O Lord, supported me.
When doubts filled my mind,
your comfort gave me renewed hope and cheer.

Psalm 94:18–19 NLT

July 27

"What's the price of a pet canary?
Some loose change, right? And God cares what happens
to it even more than you do. He pays even greater attention to you,
down to the last detail—even numbering the hairs on your head!"

MATTHEW 10:29–30 MSG

June 7

Do we think ourselves irredeemable?
Do we deny—even to God—that we have doubts
in His ability to do the impossible?
Look to the promises in God's Word.
They are for all of us, and they never fail.
"Not a single one of all the good promises the LORD
had given to the family of Israel was left unfulfilled;
everything he had spoken came true"
(Joshua 21:45 NLT).

July 26

The future is so uncertain, Lord. I find myself wishing my life away, just so I can get on the other side of this trial I am going through. A thousand different scenarios about what may or may not happen are ricocheting around in my head. Help me to find Your peace. Take my hand and lead me into Your light. Change my thoughts from panic to praise!

June 8

Abba God, I'm slipping into doubts again.
Support me with Your love—love that never fails.
Remove the doubts from my mind.
You've done it before—please, do it again!
Comfort me with Your Word. Support me on this slippery slope.
Ensure my footing. I need the cleats provided by Your promises.
They renew my hope. Oh Lord, in You alone
I surmount doubt and rise into joy.

July 25

They should seek the Lord, if haply they might feel after him, and find him, though he be not far from every one of us: For in him we live, and move, and have our being.

ACTS 17:27–28 KJV

June 9

Yes, and the Lord will deliver me from every evil attack and will bring me safely into his heavenly Kingdom. All glory to God forever and ever! Amen.

2 Timothy 4:18 NLT

July 24

"Give your entire attention to what God is doing right now,
and don't get worked up about what
may or may not happen tomorrow.
God will help you deal with whatever hard things
come up when the time comes."

MATTHEW 6:34 MSG

June 10

When doubts begin creeping back in, do not despair.
Turn them over to the Lord. Protect yourself with the shield of faith.
Arm yourself with "the sword of the Spirit,
which is the word of God" (Ephesians 6:17 TNIV).
By reciting God's promises (mentally or aloud),
you will be putting your focus back
where it belongs—on Jesus.

July 23

Everything (except our own sinfulness) comes from our Lord. "It may be the sin of man that originates the action, and therefore the thing itself cannot be said to be the will of God," Hannah Whitall Smith wrote, "but by the time it reaches us, it has become God's will for us and must be accepted as coming directly from His hands."

June 11

If you have doubts, surrender them to Jesus. Tell Him, " 'I do believe; help me overcome my unbelief!' " (Mark 9:24 TNIV). He will remind you that not only is nothing impossible for Him, that " 'no word from God will ever fail' " (Luke 1:37 TNIV), but also that "everything is possible for one who *believes*" (Mark 9:23 TNIV, emphasis added)!

July 22

Almost everything we encounter in our lives
comes to us through human instrumentalities,
and most of our trials are the result of some man or
woman's failure, ignorance, carelessness, cruelty, or sin.
But how could an all-loving God put us through such heartbreak?
We need to remember to trust Him through it all.

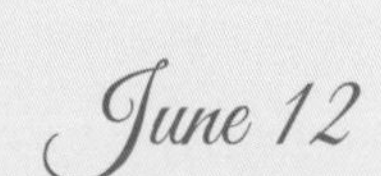

"Be strong and courageous; do not be afraid nor dismayed before the king of Assyria, nor before all the multitude that is with him; for there are more with us than with him."

2 Chronicles 32:7 NKJV

July 21

The Lord is on my side; I will not fear.
What can man do to me?

Psalm 118:6 NKJV

June 13

There is a general misconception that once we enter the life of faith, temptations and our yielding to them will cease. Another fallacy is that any temptation—whether we act on it or not—is itself a sin and that we are at fault for the suggestions of evil that entered our mind. This inevitably leads us into condemnation and discouragement, the continuing of which can result, at last, into actual sin.

July 20

Lord, I feel as if I am being tossed from floodwaters to the furnace and back again. But that's only how I feel—I know it is not reality. My reality is that You are here beside me—through fire and water. There is no need for me to freak out about anything. My comfort is that You are with me and that You will work all things out to my good. And in that fact I rest.

June 14

I feel so outnumbered, Lord. I am feeling weak and discouraged.
So I am putting all my focus on You. Give me strength and courage.
Help me to be brave before the temptations assailing me.
I am looking to You for help, knowing that
You are more powerful than anything I may ever face.
I'm putting my faith in You and You alone.
Save me, Jesus. Save me now!

July 19

Many people have confessed that although they can submit to things that come from God's hand, they have great difficulty submitting to other humans, through whom most.of their troubles come. Or they give their hearts to trusting God, but then someone comes along whose actions threaten their endeavors. We need only remember that God is by our side, 24–7.

June 15

"Because he has set his love upon Me, therefore I will deliver him;
I will set him on high, because he has known My name.
He shall call upon Me, and I will answer him;
I will be with him in trouble;
I will deliver him and honor him."

PSALM 91:14–15 NKJV

July 18

When you pass through the waters, I will be with you; and through the rivers, they shall not overflow you. When you walk through the fire, you shall not be burned, nor shall the flame scorch you.

Isaiah 43:2 NKJV

June 16

If you are facing a myriad of temptations, some stronger than others, you can know, oddly enough, that you are headed in the right direction and that God will get you through. All you need is to remain confident in Him, focused, joyful, firm in faith, patient, prayerful, planted in the Word, and steadfast in Christ.

July 17

To prevent failures and their inevitable discouragements and consequences, or to discover their causes if we find we have erred, we must make the following words our continual plea before God: "Search me, O God, and know my heart; test me and know my anxious thoughts. Point out anything in me that offends you, and lead me along the path of everlasting life" (Psalm 139:23–24 NLT).

June 17

We cannot let the fact that we're facing temptation discourage us,
but stand confident in our faith and its strength instead.
When Joshua was about to enter the Promised Land and face many foes,
God told him, "Be strong and of a good courage. . . .
Be not afraid, neither be thou dismayed. . . .
Only be thou strong and very courageous"
(Joshua 1:6, 9, 7 KJV).

July 16

If we do not confess our sins, even some innocent
or seemingly harmless habits or indulgences,
and continue to attempt to hide them from God
(an inane endeavor since He sees and knows everything),
we not only distance ourselves from God, but our misdeeds will,
like David's, take on a snowball effect until we
and perhaps others are buried by them.

June 18

Wait [expectantly] for the Lord, and He will rescue you.

PROVERBS 20:22 AMP

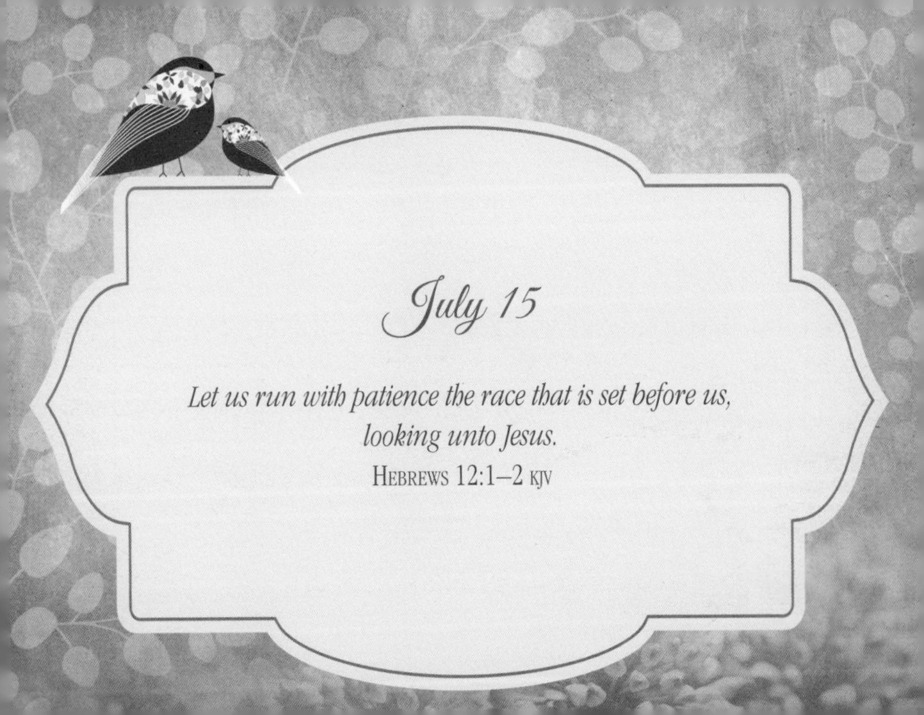

July 15

Let us run with patience the race that is set before us,
looking unto Jesus.

HEBREWS 12:1–2 KJV

June 19

Do not become discouraged when you face temptations. Instead, turn away from them and look for God to deliver you. Understand that He might not do it when or in the way you expect, for He has told us, " 'My thoughts are not your thoughts, nor are your ways My ways' " (Isaiah 55:8 NKJV). But know and understand that He will do it!

July 14

I cannot even fathom, Lord, how far away You remove our sins
from us. But I still feel so guilty and discouraged.
I want to get back up, walking in Your way. Yet my feet feel stuck.
Lift me, Lord, up and out of this pit of despair.
Help me to understand the fact that You've not only
forgiven me of my sin but have forgotten all about it.
Bring me back into Your saving grace.

June 20

I'm running out of patience, Lord.
I'm not sure how much more I can take, how much longer
I can hold on. I run to You. Shelter me in Your presence.
Be my rock and refuge—a boulder that can neither be destroyed
nor removed. I am expecting Your deliverance from temptation.
I remain steadfast in You, knowing You will rescue me.
In that fact alone, I have peace.

July 13

When we have sinned, we need to acknowledge it.
We must be like the children of Israel in this account in Joshua.
We must rise "early in the morning" (Joshua 7:16 KJV)
then run to where the sins are hidden, take them from the midst
of their hiding places, and lay them before the Lord
(see Joshua 7:22–23). Then we can stone them, burn them,
and bury them (see Joshua 7:25–26), and immediately
receive God's forgiveness, encouragement, and victory,
as did Joshua and the Israelites.

June 21

So for the sake of Christ, I am well pleased and take pleasure in infirmities, insults, hardships, persecutions, perplexities and distresses; for when I am weak [in human strength], then am I [truly] strong (able, powerful in divine strength).

2 Corinthians 12:10 AMP

July 12
As far as the east is from the west,
so far has He removed our transgressions from us.
PSALM 103:12 NKJV

June 22

Don't be brought low in your attitude, thoughts,
and demeanor in the midst of the battle.
The joy in the Lord will give you the strength you need
in the midst of your weakness (see Nehemiah 8:10).
Want to really catch the devil off guard?
When temptation whispers in your ear,
start worshipping the Lord!

July 11

As soon as consciousness of our sin has set in,
we must immediately lift up our face to God and become conscious of His forgiveness. We can only continue walking on this path of holiness by taking our eyes off our misstep and begin "looking unto Jesus" (Hebrews 12:2 KJV). Otherwise, we will keep tripping up!

June 23

Believe that His promises to fight your battles are true
(see 2 Chronicles 20:17; 32:8 for starters).
In fact, "the LORD your God walks in the midst of your camp,
to deliver you and give your enemies over to you"
(Deuteronomy 23:14 NKJV). But you must stand there with Him, for
" 'the LORD is with you when you are with Him' " (2 Chronicles 15:2 NASB).
If you suddenly can't find God, *you* are the one who has moved—not Him!

July 10

As soon as we come to Christ and confess our sins, He forgives! Immediately! There is no silent treatment, no grudge. "If we confess our sins, he is faithful and just to forgive us our sins, and to cleanse us from all unrighteousness" (1 John 1:9 KJV).

June 24

"What does the Lord *your God require of you? He requires only that you fear the* Lord *your God, and live in a way that pleases him, and love him and serve him with all your heart and soul."*

Deuteronomy 10:12 NLT

July 9

Create in me a clean heart, O God, and renew a steadfast spirit within me. Do not cast me away from Your presence, and do not take Your Holy Spirit from me. Restore to me the joy of Your salvation, and uphold me by Your generous Spirit.

PSALM 51:10–12 NKJV

June 25

To remain firm in faith, you must practice patience (see James 1:3–4). Give God time to work. He will not fail, for He has told us that "no weapon that is formed against thee shall prosper" (Isaiah 54:17 KJV). He will help you find a way out. Do not trust in yourself, for you are not strong enough.

July 8

Lord, I can no longer lie to myself. I need to come to You in truth.
My misdeed is weighing me down, Lord.
I bring it now into Your light so that You can blast it away.
Give me wisdom, Lord, to handle this situation better the next time.
Your Word says that You will help the contrite and brokenhearted, Lord.
Right now, that's me. So please, help me, heal me, make me whole.

June 26

I know that what You have done for me in the past, Lord,
You will do again. You have rescued me from temptations so many times.
And now, here we are again. You know I love You, God.
I want to live in a way that pleases You. I want to serve You—
and no one else—with all my heart, soul, and mind.
So help me again today, Lord. Fight my battles.
Give me courage to go on.

July 7

After an overwhelming failure—emotionally, physically, mentally, spiritually—we may find it easier to wallow in our despondency, our face on the ground and dust on our head, than to look up to God.
But God, as always, has a better idea.
As He told Joshua, He tells us, "Get up!"
(Joshua 7:10 NKJV).

June 27

"These things I have spoken to you, that in Me you may have peace.
In the world you will have tribulation;
but be of good cheer, I have overcome the world."

JOHN 16:33 NKJV

July 6

Behold, You desire truth in the inward parts,
and in the hidden part You will make me to know wisdom.

Psalm 51:6 NKJV

June 28

Pray. . .perhaps not so much for the removal of the temptation
but for wisdom (see James 1:5) and strength
to face it and learn from it.
Remember, God has a plan for your life,
for good and not evil.

July 5

In the beginning we may have, like babies, crawled along God's path.
But now that we are more mature in our faith, we have risen to our feet.
If we fall, we cannot lie down in discouragement and despair.
We must, like babies learning to walk, rise up and try again.

June 29

Be sure and steady in your intentions to stand firm in Christ (see James 1:6–8), for you can do all things through Christ who strengthens you (see Philippians 4:13). "For the LORD will be your confidence, and will keep your foot from being caught" (Proverbs 3:26 NKJV). So flee from the evil one and run to God. Hide beneath His wings. Do not walk out from underneath His protection by doubting. Stand still. Stand firm.

July 4

When we fail, we really have no cause for discouragement and giving up. We must recognize the fact that we are not talking about a *state* but a *walk* of life with Christ. Smith wrote, "The highway of holiness is not a *place*, but a *way*." As those hidden in Christ, we are followers of the Way.

June 30

Have mercy upon me, O God,
according to Your lovingkindness;
according to the multitude of Your tender mercies,
blot out my transgressions.
Wash me thoroughly from my iniquity,
and cleanse me from my sin.

PSALM 51:1–2 NKJV

July 3

For I acknowledge my transgressions,
and my sin is always before me. Against You, You only,
have I sinned, and done this evil in Your sight—
that You may be found just when You speak,
and blameless when You judge.

PSALM 51:3–4 NKJV

July 1

When a Christian woman embarks upon the pathway to holiness,
she may find herself suddenly and unexpectedly
encountering temptation and, before she knows it,
swept into sin. When she, like the prodigal son,
suddenly comes to her senses (see Luke 15:17),
she may then be tempted to be discouraged
and give everything up as lost or
to cover up the sin completely.

July 2

Lord, I need Your mercy. You abound in love for me, so please help me, God. Blot out the sins I have committed, the wrongs I have done. I have felt the pangs of the Holy Spirit, Lord. I am now aware of the misstep I took. My heart is so heavy. Lift me up, Lord. Help me not to wallow in discouragement but to bask in Your forgiveness that is everlasting.